The Small Museum Toolkit, Book 2

About the Series

The American Association for State and Local History Book Series publishes technical and professional information for those who practice and support history, and addresses issues critical to the field of state and local history. To submit a proposal or manuscript to the series, please request proposal guidelines from AASLH headquarters: AASLH Book Series, 1717 Church St., Nashville, Tennessee 37203. Telephone: (615) 320-3203. Fax: (615) 327-9013. Website: www.aaslh.org.

About the Organization

The American Association for State and Local History (AASLH), a national history organization headquartered in Nashville, TN, provides leadership, service, and support for its members, who preserve and interpret state and local history in order to make the past more meaningful in American society. AASLH is a membership association representing history organizations and the professionals who work in them. AASLH members are leaders in preserving, researching, and interpreting traces of the American past to connect the people, thoughts, and events of yesterday with the creative memories and abiding concerns of people, communities, and our nation today. In addition to sponsorship of this book series, the Association publishes the periodical *History News*, a newsletter, technical leaflets and reports, and other materials; confers prizes and awards in recognition of outstanding achievement in the field; and supports a broad education program and other activities designed to help members work more effectively. To join the organization, go to www.aaslh.org or contact Membership Services, AASLH, 1717 Church St., Nashville, TN 37203.

The Small Museum Toolkit, Book 2

Financial Resource Development and Management

Edited by
Cinnamon Catlin-Legutko
and Stacy Klingler

ALTAMIRA
PRESS

A Division of
ROWMAN & LITTLEFIELD PUBLISHERS, INC.
Lanham • New York • Toronto • Plymouth, UK

Published by AltaMira Press
A division of Rowman & Littlefield Publishers, Inc.
A wholly owned subsidary of The Rowman & Littlefield Publishing Group, Inc.
4501 Forbes Boulevard, Suite 200, Lanham, Maryland 20706
http://www.altamirapress.com

Estover Road, Plymouth PL6 7PY, United Kingdom

British Library Cataloguing in Publication Information Available

Library of Congress Cataloging-in-Publication Data

The small museum toolkit. Book 2, Financial resource development and management / edited by Cinnamon Catlin-Legutko and Stacy Klingler.
    p. cm. — (American Association for State and Local History book series)
    Includes bibliographical references and index.
    ISBN 978-0-7591-1949-9 (cloth : alk. paper) — ISBN 978-0-7591-1336-7 (pbk. : alk. paper) — ISBN 978-0-7591-1343-5 (electronic)
    1. Small museums—Finance. 2. Small museums—Management. I. Catlin-Legutko, Cinnamon. II. Klingler, Stacy, 1976– III. Title: Financial resource development and management.
    AM122.S63 2012
    069'.068—dc23   2011028450

♾™ The paper used in this publication meets the minimum requirements of American National Standard for Information Sciences—Permanence of Paper for Printed Library Materials, ANSI/NISO Z39.48-1992.

Printed in the United States of America

CONTENTS

EDITORS' NOTE

Small museums are faced with the enormous task of matching the responsibilities of a large museum—planning strategically, securing and managing human and financial resources, providing stewardship of collections (including historic buildings) as well as excellent exhibitions, programs, and publications, and responding to changing community and visitor needs—all with more limited human and financial resources. Small museum staff (paid or unpaid) often fulfill key responsibilities outside their area of expertise or training.

We recognize that small museum staff lack time more than anything. To help you in the trenches, we offer this quick reference, written with your working environment in mind, to make the process of becoming a sustainable, valued institution less overwhelming.

The Small Museum Toolkit is designed as a single collection of short, readable books that provides the starting point for realizing key responsibilities in museum work. Each book stands alone, but as a collection they represent a single resource to jump-start the process of pursing best practices and meeting museum standards.

If you are new to working in museums, you may want to read the entire series to get the lay of the land—an overview of what issues you should be aware of and where you can find resources for more information. If you have some museum training but are now responsible for more elements of museum operations than in your previous position, you may start with just the books or chapters covering unfamiliar territory. (You might be wishing you had taken a class in fundraising right about now!) As you prepare to tackle new challenges, we hope that you will refer back to a chapter to orient yourself.

While any chapter can be helpful if read in isolation, we suggest that you start with the first book, *Leadership, Mission, and Governance*, and look at the issues of mission, planning, and assessment. You will find that almost every chapter asks you to consider its subject in light of your mission and make decisions based on it. As you begin to feel overwhelmed by all the possible opportunities and challenges you face, assessment and planning will help you focus your scarce resources strategically—where you need them the most and where they can produce the biggest impact on your organization. And this book offers tips for good governance—defining the role of a trustee and managing the director-trustee relationship. Understanding this relationship from the outset will prevent many headaches down the road.

Financial Resource Development and Management offers you direction about how to raise and manage money and stay within your legal boundaries as a nonprofit. How to manage resources, human and inanimate, effectively and efficiently is discussed in *Organizational Management. Reaching and Responding to the Audience* encourages you to examine your museum audiences and make them comfortable, program to their needs and interests, and spread the word about your good work.

The remaining two books explore the museum foundational concepts of interpretation and stewardship in a small museum setting. *Interpretation: Education, Programs, and Exhibits* considers researching and designing exhibits and best practices for sharing the stories with your audiences. *Stewardship: Collections and Historic Preservation* rounds out the six-book series with an in-depth look at collections care, management, and planning.

We would like to thank the staff at the American Association for State and Local History and AltaMira Press, our families, and our colleagues for encouraging us to pursue this project. You have tirelessly offered your support, and we are incredibly grateful.

There is little reward for writing in service to the museum field—and even less time to do it when you work in a small museum. The contributors to this series generously carved time out of their work and personal lives to share with you their perspectives and lessons learned from years of experience. While not all of them currently hang their hats in small museums, every one of them has worked with or for a small museum and values the incredible work small museums accomplish every day. We offer each and every one of them more appreciation than we can put into words.

We hope that this series makes your lives—as small museum directors, board members, and paid and unpaid staff members—just a little bit easier. We hope that we have gathered helpful perspectives and pointed you in the direction of useful resources.

And when you are faced with a minor annoyance, a major disaster, or just one too many surprises, remember why you do this important work and that you are not alone.

It takes a very special kind of person to endure and enjoy this profession for a lifetime. Not a day passes in which I do not learn something, or find something, or teach something, or preserve something, or help someone.

—Unknown author

Keep up the good work!

Cinnamon Catlin-Legutko
Stacy Lynn Klingler
Editors

PREFACE

I have a confession to make. Until I got to the American Association for State and Local History (AASLH), I never truly understood what it was to work in a small museum. Sure, I had been around them, visited them, talked to my peers who worked in them both as paid and unpaid (read: volunteer) staff, and appreciated the role they play in the historical narrative and in communities. But I never *got it* until I got to AASLH.

So what have I learned? First and foremost, small museums are the bedrock of the American museum profession. You will not find museums the size of the Smithsonian or historic sites like Gettysburg in every American community, but you will often find a small museum, sometimes more than one. While we in the historical profession talk often about how we are the keepers of the American past, and we are, those who work in the smaller institutions are truly minders of our nation's patrimony and heritage. They care for the objects and history of communities throughout the country, stories that would probably be lost without that care. Quite simply, without small museums, our knowledge of the past, our historical narrative, would be incomplete.

The second thing I have learned, and been truly humbled by, is the passion and dedication small museum professionals and volunteers have for their craft. You will rarely hear small museum professionals complaining about a lack of resources—that is just part and parcel of the task at hand. Instead of attacking a challenge with reasons for why something cannot be done, they redirect their thoughts to how it can be done within the parameters provided. So, small museum professionals are equally comfortable with answering the phone, giving a tour, processing collections, and plunging the occasional toilet (the latter falling into the "other duties as assigned" category in a job description).

And amid all that, small museum professionals keep a great sense of humor. At several gatherings of small museum folks over the years, we have had fun with a game we call "You Know You Work in a Small Museum If . . ." Responses ranged from "A staff meeting consists of all staff members turning around in their office chairs at the same time" to "You're the director, but if you're the first one to work after a snowstorm, you get to shovel the sidewalk and plow the parking lot." But my absolute favorite was "When you walk through the gallery and hear a guest say, 'The staff should really do . . .' and you think, Hey, *I'm* my staff!"

At one time, as Steve Friesen of the Buffalo Bill Museum and Grave notes in chapter 2 of Book 1 of this series, the term *small museum* was used as a pejorative. Small museums were underfunded, under-resourced, and poorly managed. "If they weren't," the thinking went, "they'd be large museums, right?" Wrong. Being small does not mean you aspire to be big or that the institution is small because it is doing something wrong. Smallness has more to do with a spirit and dedication to a certain niche of history, a community, a person, a subject.

I believe the field has moved beyond that prejudice, and small museums are now celebrated. At AASLH we often discuss how much larger museums can learn from smaller institutions about how to serve as effective stewards of their resources and to engage their communities in a deep, meaningful way. There is much to learn from small museums, and our peers and colleagues at those institutions are ever willing to share.

Along this line, I have always found that one of the best things about the museum profession in general is how open it is with regard to sharing ideas and processes and just offering support. In no corner of the field is this more evident than in the world of small museums. Small museum professionals are founts of wisdom and expertise, and every small museum session, luncheon, or affinity event I have been to has been packed, and discussion has been stimulating and often inspiring. In fact, discussion often spills out into the hallways after the formal session has concluded.

But the work I know best is that of the AASLH Small Museums Committee. The editors of this series, Cinnamon Catlin-Legutko and Stacy Klingler, are, respectively, the founding and current chairs of this committee. Under their leadership, a team of small museum folks has completed a set of ambitious goals, including gathering a variety of research and developing a small museum needs assessment, presenting sessions at conferences throughout the country, and raising money for scholarships to send peers to the AASLH annual meeting each year. It is this last item I want to highlight as it gives the clearest example of the love and commitment those in small museums have for each other.

In my view, the fact that the Small Museums Committee successfully organizes an annual fundraising campaign is commendable. The fact that it routinely raises money to send *two* people to the meeting (and four people in some years) is truly remarkable. This is indicative of the passion and dedication small museum professionals feel toward the cause of small museums and toward their colleagues. Let's face it, history professionals are not at the top of the salary food chain. (I always note this whenever I speak to history classes about a career in public history. "If you choose this career, you are going to love what you do; you are going to be making a difference in your community. But you are also taking a vow of poverty. No one goes into the history field to get rich.") And while donors to this fund are not all from small museums, small museum professionals are a large part of the pool, giving as generously as anyone. I am so heartened each year as we raise this money.

So, what does all this have to do with the book in your hands? I would say a lot. First, the contributors are small museum professionals or aficionados themselves. They are dedicated to the craft in the small museum environment and know firsthand its needs and challenges. In addition, they have been involved with, and led national discussions on, these issues. They are passionate about the cause of small museums, and they have organized and written a book (and series) that offers a variety of voices and contexts while speaking to the needs as articulated. The thirty-plus contributors to this series offer a wealth of experience and expertise in dealing with the complex nature of running a small museum, in preserving traces of the American past for future generations, often on a shoestring budget and with limited resources. It is a lesson we can all learn. And it is a lesson well articulated here.

Whether you are a seasoned small museum professional, a newly minted executive director, or a museum studies or public history student, it is my hope that this book series will give you the tools you need to succeed in your job. I also hope that you will continue to carry the torch for small museums in your community and in the larger museum field. The field needs your passion and expertise, and the role you fill in your community is critical.

Bob Beatty
Vice President, AASLH

THE GOOD, THE BEST, AND THE IRS: MUSEUM FINANCIAL MANAGEMENT SOLUTIONS AND RECOMMENDATIONS

Brenda Granger

All museums, large and small, are encouraged to practice sound financial management—in other words, good financial control. Museums hold the public trust and should strive to maintain total transparency in their operations, including their financial operations. This transparency is defined as visible and accessible information about your museum, which includes financial information. Board oversight and accountability are at the forefront of this trust, transparency, and integrity. Maintaining sound fiscal management for the museum is a must. Ultimately, responsibility for fiscal management lies with the board of directors, and adhering to the mission of the museum is as critical as good fiscal management. This chapter does not necessarily contain original ideas but rather is a compilation of generally accepted practices, checklists, and information from respected organizations and publications, which small museums can use as a basis for making sure they have incorporated proven good financial management into their operations. Museums are encouraged to review the information and use it in their fiscal management planning and implementation. The information is meant to be general guidance on fiscal management in small museums. Museums are encouraged to consult their financial or tax advisor for specific information regarding their organization.

Stewardship in a museum takes on many forms. Examples include the stewardship of permanent museum collections, temporary exhibit loans, or financial resources. This latter stewardship will be discussed here.

The following information on stewardship has best been provided in *Hank Rosso's Achieving Excellence in Fundraising*, which quotes the *Merriam-Webster's Collegiate Dictionary* definition of "stewardship" as "the careful and responsible management of something entrusted to one's care." This definition is a good beginning. It contains the two essential components of stewardship, the concept of being responsible for something of value (nurturing or caring for it) and the recognition that what is cared for actually belongs to someone other than the caretaker (the manager or steward). We can understand stewardship, then, as being responsible for something valuable on behalf of someone who

1

has entrusted it to our care. This is not a bad way to begin thinking about the stewardship responsibility that charitable organizations have for the resources entrusted to them.

Stewardship entails more than a series of management functions, gift acknowledgment, donor recognition, prudent investment, careful accounting, and many other activities related to the fundraising process. It is all these things, of course, but also much more. Stewardship implies an even deeper burden of trust, responsibility, and accountability. It speaks to the heart of what philanthropy is; hence, it is a profound expression of the shared responsibility that individuals and organization have to contribute to the common good. Trust and responsibility are essential components of good stewardship. They are also indispensable to the concept of ethical fundraising.

Deep in the soul of any organization that wishes to practice stewardship there must be a profound awareness that the gifts it receives are to be held in trust for the public good. That is what prompts ethical organizations to acknowledge gifts and to be accountable for their use. As agents of the public good, nonprofit organizations have a special obligation to use wisely and accountably all the resources entrusted to their care. Serious regard for the trust is the soul of stewardship.[1] As with all the items discussed in this chapter, it is the responsibility of the board of directors to practice stewardship and be accountable for it.

The following checklist aims to strengthen your museum's transparency and governance and, in turn, its overall fiscal management. The steps listed in the checklist will help a museum reassure its stakeholders—donors, visitors, staff, and volunteers—of its commitment to upholding the public trust, which is vital to earning support and fulfilling its mission. The information is taken from the Independent Sector's "Checklist for Accountability" and reprinted with special permission. Independent Sector is a nonprofit, nonpartisan coalition of charities, foundations, and corporate philanthropy programs, whose mission is to advance the common good by leading, strengthening, and mobilizing the independent sector. The following list has been adapted to fit the small museum's unique characteristics.

- Your museum should develop a culture of accountability and transparency. Rules, standards, and practices are far more effective when the people they affect understand them, know why they are important, and embrace them. Teach new employees, volunteers, and board members about your principles, and give those with more experience refreshers and updates. Use your website and other communications vehicles to share examples of good behavior and policies, including your fiscal operations policies.

- Your museum should adopt a statement of values and code of ethics. This document describes the ethical principles that an organization's staff, board members, and volunteers agree to follow and includes a statement of values articulating the principles it is committed to uphold. An indispensable part of an accountable organization, a statement of values and code of ethics should be approved by the board of directors, included in staff and board orientations, and made available to the public on the organization's website.

- Your museum should adopt a conflict-of-interest policy. Adopt and enforce a conflict-of-interest policy tailored to your organization's specific needs and consistent with laws in your state. Few actions will undermine the credibility of a charitable organization faster than having its tax-exempt funds not used exclusively for charitable purposes. Adhering to a well-defined conflict-of-interest policy will help preempt even the perception that funds are being used for personal gain by managers or board members. Many states have laws that govern conflict-of-interest situations, and all organizations should consult their state laws to ensure that their conflict-of-interest policy affords them the necessary protections.

- Your museum should ensure that the board of directors understands and can fulfill its financial responsibilities. The board has the legal, as well as ethical, responsibility for ensuring the exclusive and effective use of all assets for charitable purposes. As part of this obligation, the board or appropriate board committee should review and approve all financial statements for completeness and accuracy. To perform this function effectively, the board should include individuals with financial literacy or adopt other mechanisms for drawing on independent financial expertise.

- Your museum should conduct independent financial reviews, particularly audits. Charitable organizations need to have independent reviews of their financial procedures, controls, and policies in order to provide strong financial safeguards. Charitable organizations that are required to file a Form 990 or 990-PF should determine if they should have an audit conducted of their financial statements and operations or have their financial statement reviewed by an independent public accountant.

- Your museum should ensure the accuracy of and make public the organization's Form 990. Organizations can share information about their finances and operations with charity regulators and the public using IRS forms 990-N, 990, 990-EZ, and 990-PF. To be effective, however, the information must be complete, accurate, and publicly

3

available. Be sure to have your form reviewed by the board and signed by the board president. Support efforts to improve the quality and timeliness of information about nonprofits by filing your form electronically with the IRS. Finally, be sure to post it on your website.

- Your museum should be transparent. Donors, volunteers, and staff will have much more confidence in the organization's work if they know how it is being done. Use the organization's website to share documents that provide information about finances, operations, governance, and impact.
- Your museum should establish and support a policy for reporting suspected misconduct or malfeasance (a whistle-blower protection policy). Policies and procedures that encourage individuals to come forward as soon as possible with credible information on illegal practices or violations of adopted policies are needed to protect the credibility of the organization. Employees and volunteers who identify misbehavior must feel safe to report it.

Your museum should remain current with the law. Make sure that a board member, member of the staff, consultant, or volunteer is designated to keep up-to-date with the law. Ensure that the organization fully complies with all existing laws governing charitable organizations.[2]

In addition to the items on the checklist above, museums are encouraged to implement the following as part of their sound fiscal management practices:

- Institution of an annual budgeting process
- Adherence to internal controls
- Drafting of a fiscal operations policy manual
- Accurate record keeping and compliance

Each of these items will be discussed more throughout this chapter. It is recommended to have at least one financial person on the museum's board of directors. This person can be an accountant, banker, financial advisor, or other person familiar with financial activity. If you do not currently have a financial person on your board, it is important that the board begin the process of recruiting one for future service. One other suggestion is the utilization of financial software, which is recommended for accuracy and ease of reporting. One important source of deeply discounted software is TechSoup. Through a philanthropic service called TechSoup Stock, a variety of generously donated accounting, credit card processing, and development/fundraising software is available for a modest administration fee. The TechSoup website (www.techsoup.org) lists all of the company's software partners and programs.

TEST YOUR ACCOUNTABILITY IQ

Does your museum . . .

- ❏ hold staff and board trainings on ethics or take other measures to foster a culture of accountability and transparency?
- ❏ have a code of ethics and statement of values and post them on its website?
- ❏ follow a conflict-of-interest policy and post it on its website?
- ❏ have board members with financial expertise?
- ❏ have its financial statements independently audited?
- ❏ have board members review financial statements, including the Form 990?
- ❏ have its CEO or CFO sign the Form 990?
- ❏ file its Form 990 electronically?
- ❏ post its Form 990 on its website?
- ❏ post its policies, financial information, and information on program results on its website?
- ❏ have a whistle-blower policy?
- ❏ take steps to remain current with the law?

Give your organization one point for every yes.

If your organization scores

12: Great! Keep it up and pass along your success stories and model policies so others may learn.

9–11: Good, but there's room for improvement.

6–8: There is indication of both commitment to accountability and a need to advance beyond the basics.

0–5: It is time to get serious about accountability. Engage your board, staff, and volunteers quickly to help make the needed changes.

Source: Taken from "Checklist for Accountability," Independent Sector, www.independentsector.org/checklist_for_accountability.

TEXTBOX 1.2

A RESOURCE TO KNOW

One great resource all museums should know about is the Greater Washington Society of CPAs Educational Foundation's Nonprofit Accounting Basics website (www.nonprofitaccountingbasics.org). This free resource is designed to help nonprofits produce accurate records and reports, encourage and measure accountability, and successfully manage and sustain themselves. The website has a wealth of information on such topics as starting a nonprofit, internal controls, internal reporting for good management, governance and policies, tax and filing information, audits, external reporting and disclosures, and nonprofit-specific bookkeeping and accounting. The information contained on the website is very useful for small museums. It will assist museum staff and board members in answering many financial and accounting questions, as well as provide tips, templates, and tools.

Annual Budgeting Process

It is the responsibility of the board of directors to ensure there is a budgeting process in place for the museum. A budget should not go against the museum's policies, plan for more expenses than income, or put into question the integrity of the museum. It is customary for the annual budget to be developed by both the staff and board and to cover one year of income and expenses. Some expenses will be ongoing, such as insurance, electricity, and costs for caring for the museum's collections. Other expenses will be one-off, such as special programming or a celebration event. A good starting point for budget planning is for the museum to review the outcome of past budgets and financial statements. This information can be used as a basis for budget-development discussions. The museum's strategic plan should be among the main considerations when preparing the annual budget. Some experts advise museums to add 15 percent to their budget as a contingency—in case, for example, the HVAC system needs to be fixed or, worse yet, replaced in any given year. (See table 1.1 for a sample budget form.) After the initial draft of the budget is finished, the treasurer will review it further, ask questions, and present it to the full board of directors for discussion and ultimately adoption.

After the board approves the annual budget, the staff and board manage it, and it becomes effective at the beginning of the next fiscal year. The staff and board should receive monthly computer-generated financial reports and statements from the treasurer, including comparisons to budget. The board should be ready to implement a fundraising and/or expense-reduction plan when there is a trend of expenses being greater than revenues. Maintaining a balanced budget is a must for a healthy organization.

Table 1.1. Simple Budget Example for a Small Museum

Museum Name: _____ to _____	Admin Support	Program Support	Fundraising Support	Committee Name	Committee Name	Other	Total % of Income
Income							
Grants—Projected							
Donations—Board							
Donations—General							
Donations—Annual Appeal							
Memberships							
Fundraisers (name)							
Fundraisers (name)							
Special Events (name)							
Special Events (name)							
Program (name)							
Program (name)							
Admission							
Museum Store Sales							
Miscellaneous Income							
Interest							
Total Income							

(continued)

Table 1.1. (Continued)

Museum Name: _____ Budget from _____ to _____	Admin Support	Program Support	Fundraising Support	Committee Name	Committee Name	Other	Total % of Income
Expenses							
Accounting Service (audit)							
Accounting Service (bookkeeper)							
Advertising							
Advocacy							
Bank Charges							
Board Development							
Collections Care							
Community Events							
Contract Labor							
Contributions							
Copier Rental							
Credit Card Fees							
Dues (Membership)							
Exhibits							
Food/Refreshments							
Insurance—Building							
Insurance—Employee Benefit							
Insurance—Director and Officer Liability							

Insurance—Workmen's Compensation			
Internet Services			
Maintenance (building)			
Miscellaneous			
Postage			
Printing and Copies			
Programs			
Professional Development			
Publications			
Purchase Equipment			
Purchase Retail Items			
Rental Fees			
Salaries			
Security			
Special Events and Fundraisers			
Supplies			
Taxes—Payroll			
Taxes—Sales			
Travel			
Utilities			
Total Expenses			
Net			

*Programs should be budgeted for individually and totals included in the "Program Support" column.

A number of museum board members have a hard time interpreting the numbers in financial reports. One suggestion is to incorporate instruction in how to read financial reports and the Form 990 in the new board member orientation so that all board members will be trained. The board members should be encouraged to read readily available publications on the topic and to ask questions of the treasurer or other financially savvy board members. They should not be made to feel inadequate for speaking up. Some museums even have started using a visual dashboard report or including narratives with their financial reports to assist all board members and staff with reading and understanding the financial picture. Also, museums are encouraged to keep a backup copy of the financials off-site as part of their emergency preparedness plan.

Internal Controls

Internal controls are especially important in small museums with limited staff. They should be in place to help protect staff, board members, and the organization from even the appearance, let alone the reality, of fraud or errors. A variety of internal controls have already been mentioned throughout this chapter, such as board oversight, budgeting, and policies. Other internal controls include job descriptions, check-request forms, dual signatures on checks, and, most importantly, separation or segregation of duties. These duties can be generalized into four subcategories: authorization, supervision of funds, record keeping, and reconciliation. No one individual should be responsible for all the duties, whether dealing with revenues or expenses. It is understood that many small museums do not have multiple staff members, board members, or volunteers to separate the duties, but segregating them is still both important and possible, and museums should make every effort to do so. An example of segregation of duties includes staff completing check requests, mailing checks, opening mail, and making deposits, while the treasurer approves checks, signs checks, completes deposits, and reconciles bank statements. Textbox 1.3 provides a list of internal controls.

Fiscal Operations Policy Manual

A fiscal operations policy manual should be developed to offer guidelines about the organization's financial controls and procedures. The information in the manual should be in accordance with the museum's bylaws as well as additional fiscal policy as approved by the board of directors. Although each museum will have its own specific topics in its fiscal operations policy manual, the following is a list of items that should be considered for inclusion:

- *Museum governance:* how the leadership of the museum is going to govern the organization, including processes, policies, and resources

ARE YOUR CONTROLS IN PLACE?

To help prevent fraud and control errors, here are some ways to segregate duties for cash receipts, cash disbursements, and petty cash. Adapt them for your nonprofit.

Cash Receipts
- The mail should be opened by someone other than the bookkeeper.
- Have the person opening the mail immediately stamp all checks "For Deposit Only."
- One person should run a calculator tape on checks received and keep or give them to someone other than the bookkeeper. The mail opener or bookkeeper should prepare the deposit slip.
- Someone other than the person who prepared the deposit slip should take the deposit to the bank.
- Copies of the checks should be forwarded to the bookkeeper.
- The bookkeeper should enter information into the accounting system using copies of checks.
- After the deposit is made, the validated deposit slip should be compared to the tape that was run on the checks. The person comparing these should initial the deposit slip to verify that this procedure was performed. At month's end, when the bank statement is received, this same individual should compare the deposit slips to the deposits on the bank statement.
- Acknowledgments to donors should not be prepared by the person(s) who opens the mail or by the bookkeeper.

Cash Disbursements
- Incoming vendor invoices should be forwarded to an individual who checks the invoices for addition and expense errors and then forwards them to the executive director or other responsible person for approval.
- The person approving invoices should review them in detail to confirm the charges are legitimate and initial the invoice to approve it for payment. This can be noted on the face of the invoice or on a voucher attached to the invoice.
- The approved invoice should be submitted to the bookkeeper for preparation of the check.

(continued)

TEXTBOX 1.3 (Continued)

- The bookkeeper should cancel the invoice indicating date paid and check number. The bookkeeper should then return the check and the supporting documentation to the person(s) responsible for signing checks.
- The check signer(s) should review the check, compare it to the invoice(s), review the account distribution, and sign it.
- A stamp or voucher should be used to document approval of the invoice, account distribution, the date it was paid, and the check number.
- Consider requiring two signatures on larger checks.
- Someone other than the person who prepares the checks should mail them to vendors.
- Expense reports of the executive director should be approved by a board or committee member.
- Vendors' original invoices should be matched to statements. Payment should be made based on original invoices rather than the statement.

Source: Taken from "Tools & Templates," Delaware Association of Nonprofit Agencies, www.delawarenonprofit.org/toolstemplates/managefinance_faq1.php.

- *Authority:* clarification that the board of directors has the ultimate authority but can assign authority to others within the organization
- *Internal control:* policies regarding protection of the organization from fraud and error
- *Financial planning and budgeting:* a plan for being good stewards of public funds and using resources appropriately
- *Annual budget:* policies for developing a one-year projection of income and expenses
- *Asset protection:* policy set by the board to prohibit cash from going below a certain amount
- *Financial condition:* policies regarding financial health of the organization
- *Books of account and other financial records:* policies regarding accounts kept on a cash basis or accrual basis, as well as computer generation of financial records and maintenance of a general ledger
- *Bank and other financial accounts:* policy regarding who is allowed to open and close bank and other accounts, such as certificates of deposit

- *Corporate checks:* policies regarding checks that are written on the museum's bank account
- *Withdrawal, transfer and deposit of funds:* process for removing funds
- *Deposit of funds:* process for depositing funds
- *Petty cash:* policies regarding cash kept at the museum for small, immediate needs
- *Bank and other financial account reconciliation:* policies regarding reconciliation of museum accounts
- *Accounts receivable:* policies regarding funds to be received by the museum
- *Accounts payable:* policies regarding funds owed by the museum
- *Grants receivable:* policies regarding grant funds to be received by the museum
- *Grants payable:* policies regarding grant funds owed by the museum
- *Membership dues, contributions, and other income:* policies regarding funds received
- *Capital depreciation:* policies regarding depreciation of property assets over time
- *Independent audit and federal and state reporting:* policies regarding independent professional examination of the financial statement of the museum and internal controls, as well as completion of Form 990 or similar compliance
- *Payroll and time attendance records:* policies regarding time sheets and payments to museum employees
- *Travel and expense reimbursement:* policies regarding the process for museum representatives to be reimbursed for museum travel expenses
- *Credit cards:* policy on the use of credit cards
- *Prohibiting loans:* policy prohibiting the museum from making loans to staff, members of the board of directors, or volunteers
- *Insurance policies:* annual review of all policies
- *Entering into contracts:* policies regarding who has the authority to review and sign contracts
- *Records of the museum:* policies regarding minutes from meetings of the board of directors
- *Endowment fund:* policies regarding investment of corpus in perpetuity
- *Conflict of interest:* policies regarding making sure interests do not benefit any individual
- *Whistle-blower protection:* policy for reporting of wrongful activities while protecting the individual who is reporting

- *Destruction of litigation-related documents:* time frame in which documents can be purged or destroyed
- *Indemnification:* policies for indemnifying any person associated with the museum
- *Authority to establish new or revised policy:* policies regarding how the fiscal operations policy manual can be revised

This manual will take time and effort to develop, but the organization will be better for adopting it. A sample of many of the financial policies mentioned can be obtained from the American Association of Museums's Information Center or BoardSource's *The Nonprofit Policy Sampler*.

Record-Keeping and Compliance

The Internal Revenue Service offers an array of help for small exempt organizations, including museums. Much of this information can be found on the IRS website (www.irs.gov). You are encouraged to check the website for the latest information and updates, as well as any changes in tax regulations. The following information is taken from IRS Publication 4221-PC (revised 7-2009) with a few additions and changes. Note that some legal documents may not be necessary if the museum is an agency of government, part of a public school, or property of a sovereign Indian tribe. These organizations should check with their tax advisor for further clarification and information.

When it comes to records, you may ask what records should be kept? Except in a few cases, the law does not require a special kind of record. A museum can choose any record-keeping system suited to its activities that clearly shows the organization's income and expenses. The types of activities a museum conducts determine the type of records that should be kept for federal tax purposes. A museum should set up a record-keeping system using an accounting method that is appropriate for proper monitoring and reporting of its financial activities for the tax year. If a museum has more than one program, it should ensure that the records appropriately identify the income and expense items attributable to each program. A record-keeping system should generally include a summary of transactions. This summary is ordinarily written in the museum's books (for example, accounting journals and ledgers). The books must show gross receipts, purchases, expenses (other than purchases), employment taxes, and assets. For most small organizations, the checkbook may be the main source for entries in the books, while larger organizations need more sophisticated ledgers and records. A museum must keep documentation that supports entries in the books. A museum must keep its books and records based on an annual accounting period called a tax year in order to comply with annual reporting requirements.

TEXTBOX 1.4

CASE STUDY: THE OKLAHOMA MUSEUMS ASSOCIATION WRITING A FISCAL OPERATIONS POLICY MANUAL

The Oklahoma Museums Association (OMA), as an organization, historically has practiced good fiscal management through direction of its bylaws and a variety of board-adopted policies over the years. Not until the OMA staff attended various training workshops on financial oversight and responsibility did they realize that the various fiscal management policies should all be compiled into one fiscal operations policy manual.

The first step was to gather the OMA bylaws, adopted policies, and generally accepted financial practices. The second step was to gather fiscal management best-practices information from the American Association of Museums, Independent Sector, the Oklahoma Open Meetings/Records Act, the Sarbanes-Oxley Act, Sarkeys Foundation Leadership Forum Sessions, and various sample nonprofit fiscal operations policy manuals. The third step was to make an outline of a fiscal operations policy manual and add OMA's current information to the various sections, leaving blank the sections for which OMA had no policies or practices. In these blank areas, the researched best-practice information was especially helpful, as new policies had to be written and adopted by the board of directors.

After several months, a rough draft of the OMA's fiscal operations policy manual included both the previously approved and the newly recommended policies. The rough-draft manual was submitted to a CPA for comments. The next step was to submit it to the executive committee for review and comment. Following receipt of the committee's comments, additional changes were made, items were clarified, and the fiscal operations policy manual was presented to the full board of directors for discussion and approval. It was necessary to indicate to the board in the manual which policies were already approved and in place and which policies were new and needed ratification. The board had several weeks to review the manual before the meeting at which it was to adopt it. After good discussion and a few new policy changes, the fiscal operations policy manual was approved by the full board of directors. Since its original approval, the manual has been updated as needed, with board approval.

Having a fiscal operations policy manual is of great benefit to the OMA. OMA now has an entire set of good fiscal management policies located in one easy-to-use manual. The greatest benefit is that staff and board members understand OMA's fiscal operations policies as spelled out in the manual, and the public can rest assured that OMA is a transparent and accountable organization.

For more information about accounting periods and methods, see IRS Publication 538, "Accounting Periods and Methods." Organization transactions such as contributions, purchases, sales, and payroll will generate supporting documents. These documents, grant applications and awards, sales slips, paid bills, invoices, receipts, deposit slips, and canceled checks contain information to be recorded in accounting records. It is important to keep these documents because they support the entries in books and the entries on tax and information returns. Museums should keep supporting documents organized by year and type of receipt or expense. Also, keep records in a safe place.

The next question is "Why keep records?" In general, a museum must maintain books and records to show that it complies with tax rules. The museum must be able to document the sources of receipts and expenditures reported on Form 990. If an organization does not keep required records, it may not be able to show that it qualifies for tax-exempt status or should be classified as a public charity. Thus, the organization may lose its tax-exempt status or be classified as a private foundation rather than a public charity. In addition, the museum may be unable to complete its returns accurately and, hence, may be subject to penalties described under Filing Penalties and Revocation of Tax-Exempt Status.[3]

When good record-keeping systems are in place, a museum can evaluate the success of its programs, monitor its budget, and prepare its financial statements and returns. A museum can use records to evaluate the success of its programs and determine whether the organization is achieving desired results. Good records can also help a museum identify problem areas and determine what changes it may need to make to improve performance. Without proper financial records, it is difficult for a museum to assess whether it has been successful in adhering to budgetary guidelines.

The ability to monitor income and expenses and ensure that the organization is operating within its budget is crucial to a museum's successful stewardship. It is important to maintain sufficient financial information in order to prepare accurate and timely annual financial statements. A museum may need these statements when it is working with banks, creditors, contributors, and funding organizations. Some states require public charities to make audited financial statements publicly available. Records must support income, expenses, and credits reported on the Form 990 series and other tax returns. Generally, these are the same records used to monitor programs and prepare financial statements. Books and records of public charities must be available for inspection by the IRS. If the IRS examines a public charity's returns, the organization must have records to explain items reported. Having a complete set of records will speed up the examination.

Museums may receive money or property from many sources. With thorough record keeping, a museum can identify the sources of receipts. Organizations need this information to separate program from nonprogram receipts and taxable from nontaxable income, as well as to complete schedules, including other schedules of the Form 990 series that the organization may be required to submit.

Finally, what federal information returns, tax returns, and notices must be filed? An organization should maintain a list of its donors and grantors and the amount of cash contributions or grants (or a description of the noncash contributions) received from each. An organization needs to keep records of revenues derived from, and expenses attributable to, an unrelated trade or business so that it can properly prepare Form 990-T and calculate its unrelated business taxable income.[4] The IRS has published on its website, www.irs.gov, "Form 990 Series—Filing Phase-In." Organizations are encouraged to check the IRS website for up-to-date information.

Beginning in year 2010 and later, for filing in 2011 or later, organizations with gross receipts normally $50,000 or less are required to electronically submit Form 990-N, also known as the e-Postcard, unless they choose to file a complete Form 990 or Form 990-EZ. Organizations with gross receipts normally between $200,000 and $500,000 may file the Form 990 or Form 990-EZ, and those with gross receipts over $500,000 must file Form 990. The Pension Protection Act of

---

TEXTBOX 1.5

FORM 990 CHECKLIST

The IRS has produced the "New Form 990 Preparation Checklist" to help tax-exempt organizations and practitioners prepare to file the form. The checklist includes the following:

- Determine whether you are eligible to file Form 990-EZ.
- Review the redesigned Form 990.
- Review the final instructions.
- Identify the schedules that you need to complete.
- Identify key internal stakeholders to involve in completing the form.
- Identify key external stakeholders to involve in completing the form.
- Assign an internal leader to coordinate Form 990 preparations.
- Identify your relation originations and officers, directors, trustees, and key employees.
- Be prepared to answer new questions about governance, executive compensation, and insider trading.
- Determine your overseas and joint-venture activities.
- Establish or modify internal systems to prepare for filing season.

Source: "Publication 4740 (01-2009)," Internal Revenue Service, www.irs.ustreas.gov/pub/irs-pdf/p4740.pdf (accessed February 14, 2011).

2006 added this filing requirement to ensure that the IRS and potential donors have current information about the organizations. The e-Postcard is very easy to complete. All you need is the following information about your organization:

- Employer identification number (EIN), also known as a Taxpayer Identification Number (TIN)
- Tax year
- Legal name and mailing address
- Any other names the organization uses
- Name and address of a principal officer
- Website address if the organization has one
- Confirmation that the organization's annual gross receipts are normally $50,000 or less
- If applicable, a statement that the organization has terminated or is terminating (going out of business)

Most small tax-exempt organizations with gross receipts that are normally $50,000 or less must file the e-Postcard. Exceptions to this requirement are organizations included in a group return and churches, their integrated auxiliaries, and conventions or associations of churches. If you do not file your e-Postcard on time, the IRS will send you a reminder notice, and you will not be assessed a penalty for late filing. However, an organization that fails to file required e-Postcards (or information returns such as Forms 990 or 990-EZ) for three consecutive years will automatically lose its tax-exempt status. The revocation of the organization's tax-exempt status will not take place until the filing due date of the third year.[5] Revocation is a very serious issue and would constitute an emergency in your organization. Avoid revocation by filing your e-Postcard or Form 990 or 990-EZ. It is the responsibility of the board of directors to make sure the museum is in compliance. With increasingly easy access to Form 990 on Guidestar and other websites, donors are relying on the information to determine if an organization is in compliance.

In conclusion, the fiscal management of a museum requires due diligence on the part of the museum staff and board of directors. Although it may appear daunting at first, once the organization's leadership has a basic understanding of stewardship, accountability, transparency, policies, reporting, compliance, and more, then your museum is on the high road to sound fiscal management practices. The public entrusts museums with both collections and funds, and holding this trust in the highest degree will make your institution a model of financial management success.

A RESOURCE TO KNOW

The Oklahoma Arts Council has developed a wonderful online tool, JumpstART, which is of great benefit to museums. The JumpstART financial management checklist is valuable in assessing your organization's financial management practices. The checklist is divided into two categories: organizations with budgets greater than $25,000 and organizations with budgets under $25,000.

The following checklist is recommended for organizations with budgets greater than $25,000:

- Volunteer governance
  a. Does the board of directors meet regularly?
  b. Are permanent copies of the minutes of the board meetings signed and maintained, and do they include all attachments of the reports (e.g., financial statements) presented at each meeting?
  c. Does your organization maintain signed minutes for its annual and standing committee meetings?
  d. If your organization is subject to an audit, does the board of directors review the external audit management letter and recommend corrective action where required, and are the resolutions of such weaknesses made a part of the minutes?
  e. Does your organization have an annual recognition program for its volunteers?
  f. Are training programs in place to teach all new paid and volunteer staff about your organization policies, mission, requirements, opportunities, volunteer governance and empowerment, and employment benefits?

- Human resources
  a. Does your organization have a current (e.g., produced in the last three years) written personnel policy manual?
  b. Does the personnel manual address employment issues and conditions, laws affecting staff, benefits, grievance procedures, and other items?
  c. Are separate personnel files kept for each employee?
  d. Does your organization follow standard human resources information management practices (e.g., separate medical files, employee-relation files, job files, and hiring and firing records)?

(continued)

    e. Does your organization file the appropriate payroll and withholding forms as required (see IRS Publication 15 for filing and withholding requirements, etc.)?

    f. Are all individuals handling cash transactions bonded for a reasonable amount through a dishonesty bond or crime policy?

    g. Does your organization review the adequacy of its insurance coverage, including property and liability insurance, on an annual basis?

    h. Does your organization raise sufficient funds and generate revenues to finance its budget requirements and satisfy its financial obligations?

    i. Are gross and net receipt records of a fundraising event furnished to the donor to comply with IRS requirements?

    j. Are large contributions (e.g., $250 or more) acknowledged (e.g., letters)?

    k. Is the charitable-deduction portion of a fundraising event furnished to the donor to comply with IRS requirements?

- Financial resources: administrative and accounting records
  a. Does your organization use a chart of accounts?
  b. Does your organization maintain the following accounting records:
     i. receipt book
     ii. checkbooks (or computer-printed checks)
     iii. cash receipts journal
     iv. cash disbursements journal
     v. canceled/voided checks
     vi. general ledger
     vii. paid bills
     viii. bank statements
     ix. time sheets and payroll records

- Financial resources: cash receipts
  a. Are checks restrictively endorsed immediately upon receipt?
  b. Does your organization use prenumbered receipts?
  c. Are receipts issued for all funds received?
  d. Are receipts written as soon as funds are received?
  e. Are receipts issued in chronological order?
  f. Are blank receipts properly safeguarded to ensure that only authorized persons have access to these records?
  g. Are undeposited cash and checks properly guarded in a safe or lockable, fire-resistant filing cabinet until bank deposits are made?
  h. Are cash receipts deposited intact?

    i. Are bank deposits made when the organization receives a large amount of monies, even if a deposit was prepared earlier that same day?

    j. Are funds deposited at the end of the week to keep cash from remaining in the office over the weekend?

    k. Are bank deposit slips annotated with the inclusive receipt numbers or easily reconciled with the receipt records?

- Financial resources: cash disbursements
  a. Is access to the blank-check stock limited (it should be accessible only to the check preparer)?
  b. Is the practice of signing checks to "cash" or "bearer" prohibited?
  c. Is the practice of presigning checks prohibited?
  d. Are checks signed by two authorized people?
  e. Are invoices and bills canceled by the use of a stamp or handwritten notation, including the check number and date paid, to prevent reuse and possible duplicate payment?
  f. Does your organization have adequate controls over the petty cash or change fund (e.g., surprise cash counts, disbursement support)?
  g. Does the board treasurer or another authorized volunteer not associated with the cash functions reconcile the bank statements or periodically review the reconciliations?
  h. Are reconciliations signed and dated by reconciler(s) and reviewer(s)?
  i. Are salary payrolls approved by a responsible official prior to payment?
  j. Are transfers between bank accounts or between investments properly authorized?

- Financial resources: budgets
  a. Is a board-approved organization budget developed by fiscal year?
  b. Are the budget and any revisions thereof approved by the board of directors and documented in the board minutes?
  c. Does the board investigate and take action regarding significant variances between budget and actual income or expenditures?
  d. Is this action documented in the board minutes?

- Financial resources: property and equipment
  a. Does your organization maintain a listing of its property and equipment items, including description, location, identification number, date of acquisition, and cost of each item?
  b. Do persons independent of the custody and recording functions compare property and equipment records to the items on hand on an annual basis?

(continued)

- Financial resources: financial reporting
  a. Are monthly financial reports prepared?
  b. Are financial reports reviewed monthly or at each finance committee or board meeting?
  c. Do the financial reports include both balance sheet (statement of financial position) and income statement (statement of activities) information for the reporting period, year-to-date figures, and a comparison to the budget?

The following checklist is recommended for organizations with budgets under $25,000:

- Does the board of directors meet regularly?
- Does your organization review the adequacy of its insurance coverage, including property and liability insurance, on an annual basis?
- Does your organization maintain the following accounting records:
  a. receipt book
  b. checkbooks (or computer-printed checks)
  c. cash receipts journal
  d. cash disbursements journal
  e. canceled/voided checks
  f. general ledger
  g. paid bills
  h. bank statements
  i. time sheets and payroll records
- Are checks endorsed "For Deposit Only" immediately upon receipt?
- Are cash receipts deposited intact?
- Is the practice of signing checks to "cash" or "bearer" prohibited?
- Is the practice of presigning checks prohibited?
- Are checks signed by two authorized people?
- Is a board-approved organization budget developed by fiscal year?
- Are financial reports reviewed monthly or at each finance committee or board meeting?
- Does your organization have a conflict-of-interest policy for the governing board and employees that prohibits an individual from acting in a position whereby a decision will be made concerning an organization in which the individual has substantial interest?

Source: "JumpstART: Financial Management Checklists," Oklahoma Arts Council, www.arts.ok.gov/services/js/cdjs08.html.

TEXTBOX 1.7

DOES THIS SCENARIO SOUND FAMILIAR?

The museum has a steady stream of visitors spring through fall. Its collection is based on local history, and its programming is mission based. It has a part-time, paid staff member who is busy during a twenty-hour workweek with collections, visitors, and programming. The previous treasurer had no financial management experience but did a good job keeping a detailed checkbook with supporting documents. The museum now has a volunteer treasurer who has limited financial management experience but is willing to learn. Where does the museum start practicing better fiscal management?

One Possible Solution
First, the paid staff member should free up some of his or her time to be more involved in the financial management. This can be accomplished by recruiting additional volunteers or asking board members to assist with collections, visitors, or programming. The staff member and the new treasurer should learn what good financial management entails for a museum. They should start by utilizing the resources found at the end of this chapter. Professional development courses and books in understanding financial management are essential at the beginning of the process. They should also refer to the IRS website to determine which forms they need to be filing to be in compliance. They should determine which policies and procedures already have been put in place and which need to be adopted. Although they have a good record-keeping system in place, other policies need to be reviewed or adopted, including internal controls and whistle-blower protection.

The treasurer should then submit the new policies and procedures regarding all aspects of fiscal management to the board for approval. They should inform other board members and volunteers that the museum is becoming accountable and transparent in all financial matters.

The next step is to adopt a code of ethics and conflict of interest. Samples can be found on the websites of the Association of Fundraising Professionals (www.afpnet.org) and the American Association of Museums (www.aam-us.org), as well as at other locations.

After this adoption is complete, board members are educated on how to read and understand financial statements. At the end of the fiscal year, an independent public accountant should conduct a review of the financial procedures, controls, and policies. Next, Form 990 should be filed and a copy made available for public inspection. This will assist with transparency.

Finally, the staff and treasurer must remain current with the law, which means subscribing to e-mail lists with the latest information as well as having an informed museum staff and/or volunteers. The staff member and board will need to work closely together on the fiscal management process. It could take a year (or more) to complete all these steps, but doing so will be well worth it for the overall health of the organization.

Resources

American Association of Museums (www.aam-us.org): code of ethics, information center, and much more helpful information

Association of Fundraising Professionals (www.afpnet.org): code of ethics and the accountable nonprofit organization

Blue Avocado (www.blueavocado.org/category/topic/finance-strategy): nonprofit finance and strategy

BoardSource (www.boardsource.org): website dedicated to advancing the public good by building exceptional nonprofit boards and inspiring board service

Charity Navigator (www.charitynavigator.org): the nation's largest and most utilized evaluator of charities

CharityChannel (www.charitychannel.com): leading source of original articles and book reviews that are down-to-earth, practical, and relevant to the day-to-day challenges of in-the-trenches nonprofit professionals

Charity Village (www.charityvillage.com/cv/research/rlegal17.html): article titled "Nonprofit Fraud: Focus on Segregation of Duties and Good Reporting Procedures

CPA Journal (www.nysscpa.org/cpajournal/old/14465853.htm): article on internal controls

Financial Accounting Standards Board (www.fasb.org)

Governmental Accounting Standards Board (www.gasb.org)

Greater Washington Society of CPAs Educational Foundation Nonprofit Accounting Basics (www.nonprofitaccountingbasics.org)

Guidestar (www.guidestar.org): website that gathers and publicizes information about nonprofit organizations

Idealist.org (www.idealist.org): policies for financial accountability

Independent Sector (www.independentsector.org): leadership forum for charities, foundations, and corporate-giving programs committed to advancing the common good in America and around the world

Internal Revenue Service (www.irs.gov/charities): tax information for charities and other nonprofits

National Council of Nonprofits (www.councilofnonprofits.org): network of state and regional nonprofit associations serving more than twenty thousand member organizations

Nonprofit Issues (www.nonprofitissues.com): nonprofit law you need to know

Quality 990 (www.qual990.org): website encompassing a number of projects and activities to improve the quality of IRS Form 990 reporting by nonprofit organizations

Standards for Excellence Institute (www.standardsforexcellenceinstitute.org/NewAuditingStandards.html): new auditing standards and how they may impact your organization

TechSoup (www.techsoup.org): website offering nonprofits a one-stop resource for technology needs by providing free information, resources, and support, including discounted software

Notes

1. Daniel Conway, "Practicing Stewardship," in *Hank Rosso's Achieving Excellence in Fundraising*, ed. Eugene R. Tempel, 2nd ed. (San Francisco: Jossey-Bass, 2003), 432.

2. "Checklist of Accountability," Independent Sector, www.independentsector.org/issues/accountability/Checklist/Checklist_Full.pdf (accessed November 4, 2009).

3. "Compliance Guide for Tax Exempt Organizations," Internal Revenue Service, http://www.irs.gov/pub/irs-pdf/p4221nc.pdf (accessed August 14, 2011).

4. "Publication 4221-PC (revised 7-2009)," Internal Revenue Service, www.irs.gov/pub/irs-pdf/p4221pc.pdf (accessed November 4, 2009).

5. "Annual Electronic Filing Requirement for Small Exempt Organizations—Form 990-N (e-Postcard)," Internal Revenue Service, www.irs.gov/charities/article/0,,id=169250,00.html (accessed November 6, 2009).

FEARLESS FUNDRAISING: A ROADMAP FOR KICK-STARTING YOUR DEVELOPMENT PROGRAM
Cinnamon Catlin-Legutko

Time and time again, in meeting after meeting, fundraising is a topic for small museum leaders that often inspires anxiety and frustration. It does not have to be this way. Fundraising is about sharing a story you are passionate about with someone with similar interests. That is all. If you believe in the mission and have a little training in fundraising techniques, you can transform yourself from a hesitant participant into a dynamic fundraiser.

Board members and staff need to understand a few well-proven facts as they evaluate and plan for current and future fundraising or development efforts (e.g., membership and annual fund drives, capital and endowment campaigns, planned giving, and major gifts):

- Individual giving is the cornerstone of nonprofit annual and major giving. In 2009, 75 percent of the charitable gifts to nonprofit organizations came from individual donors, with only 13 percent coming from foundations, another 8 percent from bequests, and 4 percent from corporations.[1]
- Of the total giving in 2009, only 4 percent went to arts, culture, and humanities (the sector in which museums and history organizations show up). The largest sector, religion, received 33 percent of the contributions. Of particular note, education is second at 13 percent.[2] The more connected you are with K–12 education, the more eligible you are for a bigger piece of the funding pie.
- On average, 80 percent of the dollars comes from 20 percent of your donor base. Despite this, both groups require your attention, but in different ways.
- A large first gift is very rare. With caring stewardship, combined with appropriate solicitation methods, identifiable segments of the membership base will move up the donor ladder toward larger and larger gifts. This process is a natural progression—a continuum—for our solicitation efforts and our donors.

- Donors must be an involved constituency and care about the service you provide.
- The board must be the vanguard of those supporting the museum. Board members must participate 100 percent in the giving program at the highest level each can support. Major gifts usually come in large part from the board and their relationships.

It is also important to note that diversified income streams are critical to the sustainability of any organization. If one revenue source is negatively impacted by external or internal forces, then the others can pick up the slack in a given budget cycle.

Because individuals comprise 75 percent of the charitable giving pool, this chapter focuses primarily on practical approaches to asking individuals to donate. When asked the secret of her success, Blithewold Mansion's executive director, Karen Binder, stated that "fundraising is about developing relationships. I think we've been successful at Blithewold because those who donate are made to feel special, and we've used their gifts to make continuous improvements and investments into the property." If individuals are the primary donors, building strong relationships is critical, and you need a careful and thoughtful fundraising strategy.

Getting Started

Every community has a philanthropic pattern. Some small communities have one or two major donors who believe in the type of work a museum does, and their support for the organization offers a seal of approval that encourages other donors. Some communities may have a plethora of nonprofits competing for just a few funding sources. And in other communities, philanthropy is deeply embedded, and community members are willing to support a number of nonprofits. Whatever the giving culture in your area, it is important to understand it and pay attention to who the donors are and where their giving is going.

Before you begin planning and implementing your fundraising strategies, it is critical to conduct an assessment of your community. To do this, gather knowledgeable community members together for a meeting, dedicate a board meeting for a fulsome discussion, and interview stakeholders and ask questions about funding sources and recent projects in the community that benefited from philanthropy. (See textbox 2.1 for sample questions to help you assess your community's philanthropic culture.) A casual conversation, with a volunteer scribe to document each of these meetings, will create numerous leads and help clarify strategy. You might also look for an impartial, volunteer facilitator from within the community to help with the conversations (colleges, universities, and extension offices are regular sources for this type of person).

SAMPLE QUESTIONS FOR ASSESSING PHILANTHROPIC CULTURE

1. How many nonprofit organizations are in the community? What percentage is actively fundraising?
2. How are peer organizations (i.e., other museums in the community) funded?
3. Which are the most generous businesses and corporations in the community? How do they like to give (e.g., via direct funding, volunteering time, making in-kind gifts of materials and services)?
4. Are there one or two philanthropists in the community? Where do they like to give their money?
5. If there are other museums in the community, do they have strong individual support?
6. How many grant-making agencies and foundation give to your community? Where are they located, and what is their giving focus?
7. What is the per capita income of the community?[1]

Note

1. Reviewing U.S. census data is very informative and will tell you how scarce financial resources are for community members (i.e., poverty rates, educational achievement, population age, etc.).

From these conversations, you may also indentify people who can help you (i.e., development committee members, future board members, and donors).

At this early stage, forming a development committee to help you is a good idea. If you decide to do so, articulate the roles and responsibilities of the committee members ahead of time and be sure to communicate this information in written form. You should also establish meeting frequency and stick to the schedule. This committee will be the primary fundraising arm of the organization, although the board will have key parts in the process. It will also be the group that helps you develop a fundraising plan. (See textbox 2.3 for more information about working with a development committee.)

Making a Plan

Now that you understand the philanthropic nature of your community, it is time to put your plan to paper. To be effective, this plan needs to identify all sources

THE BLITHEWOLD FUNDRAISING STORY

Situated on Narragansett Bay in Bristol, Rhode Island, Blithewold Mansion, Gardens, and Arboretum is a thirty-three-acre historic garden estate. The property features several historic gardens, a diverse collection of mature specimen trees (including the largest giant sequoia east of the Rockies), the Van Wickle family's entire collection of furniture, art, and decorative objects, and archives dating from the mid-1800s.

Though Blithewold is not technically a small museum as characterized in *The Small Museum Toolkit* series,[1] its fundraising prowess is inspiring to any small museum looking to ramp up fundraising. And when the property initiated the organizational transformation that stabilized its finances, it went from zero to fifty mph nearly overnight.

In 1998, the property was in financial crisis, and its owner, the Heritage Trust of Rhode Island (now Preserve Rhode Island), explored stewardship solutions. A committed group of citizens banded together to "save" the property from developers, keeping it open for public access. In this urgent state, they raised $650,000 in a few short weeks to cover operating costs, and the site has flourished ever since because of a solid commitment to fundraising and earned income strategies (over 70 percent of the budget is earned income!).

When asked about the fundraising strategies used at Blithewold, Executive Director Karen Binder shared,

> Our approach is very personal. I take the time to personalize every membership renewal letter and annual fund letter with my signature, and I write a short note alongside my name. Then, a few years ago, we instituted a policy that either a board member or I call any donor that gives more than $100 to the organization to thank them personally for their contribution. If a donor contributes more than $500, he or she receives an invitation to join me for a walk through the gardens. While many donors decline my invitation because of time restraints, I know they appreciate the gesture, and it has built loyalty over the years.

Operating today with seven full-time staff, this large site also benefits from the help of over two hundred volunteers and some part-time staff. Because Blithewold keeps the organizational staffing relatively lean, the money raised has either built the endowment (it was $0 in 1998, and it is $3.8 million in 2010 with an additional $1 million in a charitable remainder

(continued)

trust) or been invested in the property. In 2000, the operating budget was $627,000; in 2006, it was $900,000. In 2010, the operating budget was $1.2 million. This is growth by leaps and bounds sustained by aggressive and consistent fundraising strategies. To learn more about Blithewold, visit www.blithewold.org.

Note

1. In 2007, the Small Museums Committee of the American Association of State and Local History established the definition that guides this book series. A small museum's characteristics are varied, but they typically have an annual budget of less than $250,000, operate with a small staff with multiple responsibilities, and employ volunteers to perform key staff functions. Other characteristics, such as physical size, collections size and scope, and so forth, may further classify a museum as small.

of income that the museum will pursue, and it is a good idea to have your board members formally approve it and review status reports regularly. This will remind everyone of his or her fundraising duties and alert board members to progress. It will also serve as an educational tool for new and inexperienced board members. Each section should identify who is responsible for any actions identified and can include a status section for reporting. There is no prescriptive time line for a fundraising plan—it can be ongoing with regular updates, or a new one can be developed every few years. At the end of this chapter (textbox 2.9), I offer an outline for your plan, but be sure to adapt it to the needs of your organization.

Developing Your Case Statement

The need for funding is always present in museums. As members of the non-profit sector, museums compete in a universe of worthy and established non-profits[3] that are charged with making the world a better place. To be heard in all of this noise, your organization must make a case for itself. Usually small museums' most serious funding need is operating support; yet very few foundations, corporations, or donors find this a compelling reason to give. Fortunately, you can convince them with a clearly articulated strategic or long-range plan.

The strategic plan charts your museum's path over the next three to five years with an eye toward sustainability and growth. This can easily be adapted into a case statement or many statements, depending on the funding source and current goals of the museum. And many grant makers require a strategic plan, as it demonstrates that the organization is committed to success and is accountable to the community. To learn how to develop such a plan, refer to

A WORD ABOUT DEVELOPMENT COMMITTEES

Typically, development committees are part of a museum's governance structure, and many consultants and peer assessors will recommend forming one to support the fundraising actions of the board. However, it is very easy for board members to shunt their fundraising role to the committee and forget that bringing resources to the organization is a primary responsibility for board members. And it is very easy for a committee to get stuck or overstep boundaries without clear purpose.

Unless your board has a proven track record of universal participation in fundraising activities, you need a development committee with a chair or chairs who are focused on engaging their board peers. How that committee operates depends on the museum's staffing structure. If you are a small museum with one employee, you need all the help you can get, and a properly functioning committee will help. If you have someone on staff, in addition to the director, responsible for fundraising, a committee may not be needed as much. Instead, that staff member, or director of development, will work with specific board members as fundraising visits are made. This structure is possible with only one employee as well.

If you decide that you need a development committee, a clear job description is required at the outset. Here is a sample committee overview:

The development committee leads the fundraising efforts of the organization. Although fundraising is the responsibility of all board members, the committee is responsible for setting the policies and expectations, planning the donor approach, coordinating leads, facilitating and implementing direct asks, and making a case to the community. Committee members may include board members, members of the executive committee, and other individuals not yet engaged on the board, such as members or volunteers.

As you develop the description, it would be a good idea to outline fully what roles the committee will fulfill in the fundraising plan. Whatever you do, be very clear about what everyone's roles and responsibilities are and give them deadlines. Small museums are often shackled by a lack of action in the development arena.

chapter 4, "DIY Strategic Planning," in Book 1 of this series, *Leadership, Mission, and Governance.*

The executive director of the Mount Desert Island Historical Society, Tim Garrity, shared how that organization's recently approved three-year strategic plan is making a case to the community.

> The plan identifies a commitment to increase their work as historians—to "promote and preserve the historic significance of Mount Desert Island—its people and sense of place—through our collections, scholarship, and programs." With the belief that a clear focus on scholarship is essential to fundraising effort, the board and staff want to create an environment that is conducive to historical research by scholars, interns, families, and others. The results of this research will be published in our annual journal, *Chebacco*, newsletters, and online media.

In some instances, you will have a clearly defined project—an educational program, a temporary exhibit, a collaborative initiative—that you can match to funders' giving interests and priorities. Whether you are making a case for the strategic plan or a stand-alone project, the components of a good case statement are simple: Outline the purpose of the organization, describe your project and why it meets community needs, and demonstrate the project's planned impact on the community. And to add resonance, include a brief anecdotal story that illustrates the impact of your organization and your project.

Once you have expanded on these components, neatly format the text as a one- to two-page document (requirements may vary) and pair it with supporting documentation. If you are meeting with an individual, all of this information can be neatly bundled in a two-pocket folder with a small sampling of your marketing materials (i.e., rack card, education brochure, press clippings).

Now you have a source document that you can mine for a fundraising letter or use in total for a formal presentation to a donor.

It Begins with Membership

Every nonprofit concentrates on building its donor base—from the $5 to the $100 donor, there is typically a large contingent of supporters who give fairly regularly at modest levels. In the museum world, memberships constitute the base of support—a pool of individuals who have the potential to make larger gifts to the annual fund and beyond. This is not to say that all donors are members; oftentimes, the membership program does not show up on a major donor's radar. For the regular museumgoer, membership programs are well known and are a great way to engage with an institution and receive benefits.

Benefit programs vary, and you can work with your development committee to generate creative ideas with minimal cost impact for the organization. A

TEXTBOX 2.4

FOUNDATION LETTERS OF REQUEST

The process you went through to develop a case statement is the same as that for developing an effective letter of request to a foundation. However, before you spend time drafting a letter, do a little research.

Charitable foundations will share information about how to make a funding request on their websites, or you can contact the office directly by letter or phone call. Many states publish a grant-maker resource book[1] that documents grant-making activity in your state. This invaluable research tool will tell you how to apply to a certain foundation. As you do your research, track the information in a simple spreadsheet:

Foundation Name	Application Deadline	Funding Focus	Application Process	Contact Information	Notes/Status
XYZ Foundation	April 1	Youth, education	One page letter of request	Jane Smith, phone, e-mail	Letter submitted
ABC Foundation	Rolling	Arts and culture	One page letter of request, recent audit, proof of nonprofit status, list of board members	Bob Jones, phone	Declined; encouraged to apply again next year

Before submitting a letter, do your best to talk with someone in the foundation office about your proposal to confirm that it meets the foundation's funding criteria and to understand how competitive the application process is (i.e., what percentage of applicants is funded each year).[2] And if you know someone who sits on the foundation board, drop that person a note to alert him or her to your incoming letter of request. A board member or museum friend can do this as well, which has more impact.

Now that you've collected all the information, your letter can be constructed in the same way as your case statement: organizational purpose, project description, description of need and impact, and a "warm-and-fuzzy" anecdote.

Notes

1. For example, in Indiana it is called the *Directory of Indiana Grantmakers*, published by the Indiana Grantmakers Alliance, and in Maine it is called the *Maine Directory of Grantmakers*, published by the Maine Philanthropy Center.

2. You may be shocked to find that the most publicized charitable foundation in your state is able to give to only a few. I had been encouraged time and again to apply to a very well-known foundation in Maine, but after a conversation with a staff person, I learned that only 10 percent of applicants are funded each year. As I balance my time, I have to consider whether this is worth it. Fortunately the foundation requires a simple letter of request, but, not surprisingly, I was not awarded. Based on the amount of time you have to devote to writing, you may make the call that it is not worth the investment for such a slim chance.

robust benefit program is one of the best ways to attract members, and many people need something tangible for their money. While memberships are not the most lucrative way to attract income, they provide the first connection to an individual and an opening for sharing the museum's story and goals.

In 2003, the General Lew Wallace Study & Museum (GLWSM) in Crawfordsville, Indiana, started a new chapter of its story. Community leaders and board members wanted to transform from a locally known but static historic site about General Lew Wallace into a well-known, professionally operated, and dynamic National Historic Landmark. I was hired as the organization's first professionally trained museum director, and in six short years, we posted remarkable visitation, budget increases, and program attendance numbers, culminating in the National Medal for Museum Service in 2008. We covered a lot of ground incredibly fast because we did two things: We developed and implemented an aggressive strategic plan, and we got serious about fundraising. Our strategic planning methodology is well documented in "DIY Strategic Planning" in Book 1. Our fundraising strategy follows the steps outlined in this chapter, and it began with our membership program.

For a number of years, there had been a membership program at GLWSM, but by 2003, renewal mailings were inconsistent, and a benefit program was nonexistent. To help us kick-start the new membership program, we hired an independent consultant who had fundraising experience in small Indiana communities like ours. This was important because she understood the philanthropic culture very well and could deftly guide us to a membership program that was scaled to our capacity. In other words, we could deliver what we promised.

We began by determining the appropriate price point for membership in Crawfordsville—$25 for an individual membership[4]—and developed a ladder of benefits and giving up to $500. Each membership level was assigned a name that reflected our mission and history (we included these history nuggets in the brochure), and the benefits listed were suitable to the level of giving. The original benefits ladder is included in textbox 2.5, and as of this writing, it is still in use today.

A membership brochure is an effective way to share your mission and the benefits of the membership program. It is also a clever idea to design the brochure so that it doubles as a reply envelope. Whether an individual picks the brochure from a rack or receives it inside a mailing, he can easily fill out the membership form, slip a check in the envelope, and drop it in the mail back to you.

Of course, once you have done all this work, you want to increase your membership ranks as well as renew existing members. The board members and development committee can be of great assistance by submitting names and addresses from their personal address books, business contact list, holiday mailing list, social groups, professional groups, and so forth. Whatever sources they are willing to share, you need to be ready to capture the addresses in a database like PastPerfect. Depending on your museum's financial ability, you can also buy mailing lists.

That first mailing should go to any existing members with information announcing the new program and inviting them to renew within the new structure. If you have not instituted a major dues increase, most people will renew without a blink. From this point, you will need to establish a regular renewal schedule. There are many schools of thought about how frequently renewals should be sent. I am a fan of monthly mailings—they keep income flowing throughout the year and force you to keep a close eye on your members and the attrition rate. If you are using a suitable database, generating your renewal mailing list can be a snap.

The body of your renewal letter needs to make as strong a case for support as an acquisition letter (new member request). The letter will explain why the member should renew, describe some of the exciting things planned for the upcoming year, and highlight recent successes. Remember, you probably have a lovely case statement lying around that you can adapt for this letter (hint, hint). It is advisable to encourage renewing members to upgrade their membership levels. Most importantly, you should always ask for gifts in a specific amount.

Individuals should be asked to renew no more than three times over the course of three months. The first two letters can be from the director with the third from the board president. If there is no response, stop mailing letters, but do not remove the individual's information from your database. A member may return in the future, and you will want to maintain a continuous record of their giving. I also urge you to use your discretion about renewal mailings. If you

TEXTBOX 2.5

GENERAL LEW WALLACE STUDY & MUSEUM MEMBERSHIP BENEFITS

Ben-Hur Level: $500 or More
The book *Ben-Hur*, written by General Lew Wallace, is probably his most remembered accomplishment.

- One punch pass for two rounds of eighteen-hole golf at the Crawfordsville Municipal Golf Course or a one-month family pass to the Crawfordsville Community Center
- Once-a-year complimentary use of grounds
- Exclusive invitations to two selected museum special events
- Complimentary admission for two to the museum for a year
- A 10 percent discount in our gift shop
- Subscription to our quarterly newsletter

Ambassador Level: $250
On May 18, 1881, General Wallace was appointed U.S. minister resident to the Ottoman Empire by President James A. Garfield.

- Once-a-year complimentary use of grounds
- Exclusive invitations to two selected museum special events
- Complimentary admission for two to the museum for a year
- A 10 percent discount in our gift shop
- Subscription to our quarterly newsletter

Governor Level: $100
In September 1878, General Wallace was appointed governor of the New Mexico Territory.

- Exclusive invitations to two selected museum special events
- Complimentary admission for two to the museum for a year
- A 10 percent discount in our gift shop
- Subscription to our quarterly newsletter

Major General Level: $50
Lew Wallace was commissioned major general of U.S. volunteers on March 21, 1862. On July 9, 1864, he fought a battle at Monocacy that saved the city of Washington, DC, from capture by Confederate forces.

(continued)

- Complimentary admission for two to the museum for a year
- A 10 percent discount in our gift shop
- Subscription to our quarterly newsletter

Lieutenant Level: $25
When the Mexican-American War began, Lew Wallace entered the service on June 18, 1846, as a second lieutenant.

- Complimentary admission for two to the museum for a year
- Subscription to our quarterly newsletter

At the bottom of the benefits ladder, whether listed in the brochure or on the website, it is important to list actual costs. Donors are not able to deduct membership dues if there is an exchange of goods equal to the value of the gift. In this example, if I became a member at the Major General Level, I could only deduct $46.

For tax purposes, we have provided the market value of your benefits: Lieutenant Level = $4, Major General Level = $4, Governor Level = $4, Ambassador Level = $54, *Ben-Hur* Level = $85.

know that someone values his membership and regularly attends programs, but you cannot get him to renew, take a break from the renewal mailings (maybe six months) and then send a new renewal request. Sometimes renewals arrive when members are really busy, out of town, or sick, and they are slow to respond. It may not mean they are dissatisfied with your museum. Be patient, and you will be rewarded.

Once your renewal process is routine, set the date for a membership drive. Preferred months for membership drives are May (a fair distance from tax season) and October (for end-of-year giving). Draft a one-page letter that distills the case statement into a concise and compelling letter of appeal. Paired with the reply brochure, this letter will be mailed to the prospect list you have been compiling.

At GLWSM, we posted above-average returns because the community had not heard from us before, we assembled an excellent mailing list (most people on the list had interest and capacity), and we shared a compelling vision for the future. Our first membership drive was in 2004, followed by a second drive in 2005. The first drive netted over a 20 percent return rate, and the second was closer to 15 percent (for approximately two thousand letters mailed). The rule

TEXTBOX 2.6

THE MOUNT DESERT ISLAND HISTORICAL SOCIETY'S FUNDRAISING STORY

Founded in 1931, the Mount Desert Island Historical Society in Mount Desert, Maine, works to preserve the history of Mount Desert Island (MDI) and the surrounding region. The society produces changing exhibits in four museum buildings on the island, the most iconic of which is the Selectman's Building and Bridge, one of the most photographed sites on MDI. This location is in the center of the island in Somesville, which was settled in 1761 as the first permanent European settlement on MDI.

Many of the area's most important historical artifacts and archives are held in a four-hundred-square-foot, climate-controlled archival storage area, totaling over nine thousand items. With one full-time staff person, the executive director, a team of volunteers works approximately eighteen hours per week cataloging the collection. The oldest item in the collection is the Somes powder horn, dated 1770, an artifact owned by Abraham Somes, the first permanent European settler.

Operating in 2011 with a budget of over $96,000, the society raises 40 percent of its budget through membership dues.

Income Source	Amount	Percentage
Membership	$39,000	40
Donations	$15,100	17
Grants	$10,000	10
Major gifts	$10,000	10
Other	$22,500	23
Total	$96,600	100

When asked about the society's fundraising efforts, Tim Garrity, executive director, shared its three primary strategies:

We've tried to establish fundraising as a value exchange: scholarship in exchange for giving. Our first strategy is content based. We think by producing good content, we enhance our credibility and value as a historical organization. And, that this value will be appreciated and rewarded by donors. We want to distribute historical content and make it readily accessible across multiple media platforms, and then ask donors to give based on their perception of the value and importance of the work.

(continued)

39

Our second strategy is process based. We want to establish routine processes to encourage giving and membership. These processes include good database management, making the best use of our member-management software, scrubbing the data to assure that names, addresses, and mail-merge letter templates are of high quality, and thoughtfully conducting each phase of the gift process, including solicitation, receipt, and acknowledgment.

Our third strategy is relationship based. We've asked our board members to each name ten prospective new members as part of a systematic new-member drive. Each new-member prospect receives a letter, with a marginal note from the board member, encouraging them to join the society. We're trying to expand our connections in the community based on personal relationships with our board. We've also established development expectations for the board, asking that they give a minimum of $1,000 either by direct donation, or in-kind donation of time, or by finding new donors.

The results are already paying off. In two years, the society has experienced a 225 percent increase in annual contributions and membership dues! To learn more about the Mount Desert Island Historical Society, visit www.mdihistory.org.

of thumb for the return on direct mail appeals is 1 percent. We were obviously excited about the results! However, the October 2006 mailing netted a 2 percent return rate, and the mailing list appeared exhausted. After this drop-off, we discontinued large mailings (financial savings) and transitioned to smaller, more frequent mailings to "warm leads." This included mailings to the visitor register (sent within one month of a person's visit), board referrals, and other mailing lists. We also collected prospect names during our museum events (we circulated a clipboard with a sign-up form for more information) and through direct observation at our events. If you see people return time and again to your programs and they are not yet members, they need to be asked![5]

Beginning in 2006, we held cultivation parties, or house parties, to recruit new members. Board members and museum friends would invite potential members to their homes for a casual gathering. The invitations would make it clear that guests were invited to hear about the exciting events at the museum. Once guests had arrived, the host would provide food and drink, and I, as the museum director, would take just a few moments to share the good word about the museum and make a pitch for membership.[6] During this segment, the host would circulate membership brochures. These small, intimate gatherings usually resulted in two to three new members. This may sound like a great deal of time spent, but if the host is covering all the costs and identifying a guest list, the staff time is minimal, and the good will promoted has a ripple effect in the community.

As you acquire new members, it is equally important to work hard to retain them. With the receipt of the first gift, a formal thank-you letter is sent that highlights some of the museum's accomplishments and reiterates the level of gift given. This letter acts as a receipt and gives proper acknowledgment of the gift. Ideally, thank-you letters should be issued within the first twenty-four to forty-eight hours after receipt of a gift. If the gift is significant, it is a good idea to thank the donor personally with a phone call.

You can keep the excitement and membership benefits alive in between renewal cycles by building a "club" mentality among the members. This makes them feel a connection to each other and to the museum. An annual party can be held to thank donors and members for their generosity and support. Party invitations can be listed as one of the benefits of membership. Donor sneak preview parties for exhibit openings are also extremely popular.

Annual Giving and Major Gifts

Building an annual fund is essential for building a budget. Recall that memberships often have a higher cost associated, making the gift not fully tax deductible (in some organizations, the cost of benefits equals the membership price). As the organization grows and fulfills its mission, the need for operating income will increase. Asking for an annual gift helps balance the budget and provide for a sustainable future.

The annual fund provides critical support to every aspect of the museum's programs and operations. It bridges the gap between admissions, museum store sales, special event revenues, and the actual cost of running the museum and its programs. Funds from the annual fund are typically unrestricted and can be requested by direct mail and in face-to-face meetings. In addition, special events can raise money for the annual fund. Be careful not to accidentally restrict donations to the annual fund by being too specific about how you will use the money.

Annual fund donors are usually identified from the existing membership, but they are also in the larger community and visiting populace. The dynamics of giving follow three routes to your organization: linkage, ability, and interest. A linkage is a member or a donor to the collection and so forth. Ability is simply having the wealth to make a gift. Research will determine how able the individual is. And lastly, an interest or inclination toward the organization makes the "ask" more "warm." Two of these dynamics, linkage and interest, can be changed.

To change and improve linkages and interests, the development committee should work in the community spreading the message for the museum and building confidence in the organization. Inviting people to the museum for a personal tour with the director or curator is a great way to orient potential donors to your mission. Invite them back to see an educational program in action. For Blithewold, a few committed board members assist the executive director in development efforts. "One in particular enjoys fundraising, and he takes the initiative to invite prospective donors and foundation leaders to the property regularly. We walk the individual through the gardens, provide project updates, financial updates, and then sit either in the mansion's dining room or on the porch and enjoy lunch or tea. It's been very effective for our organization." The strategic plan, case statement, direct mailings, member parties, and personal interaction will provide all the contact and discussion points for this effort.

After two years of successful membership acquisition and renewal, you are ready to ask people to give to the annual fund. The direct mail piece is typically a one-page letter that makes the case for support and distinguishes itself from membership. To set it apart further, you may want to have your board president or the annual fund chair (this can be a board member) sign the letter of request. If written from that signer's point of view as to why she gives, it is all the more convincing. You will need to produce a card enclosure, or reply device, to insert with the letter along with a self-addressed envelope. Ideally, this appeal will go out two to three times per year with a new message. You can count a request for donations in your newsletter as an appeal.

At GLWSM, we started our membership campaign in 2003, with the results reported above. The first annual fund appeal was mailed in December 2005 and continued each year, netting between $9,000 and $12,000 in unrestricted funds (this was 7 to 10 percent of the total budget). Ideally, as your donor base grows, so will the income from the annual appeal.

After a few years of a regular annual appeal process, it is a good idea to sit down with your development committee and consider a major gifts program. A major gift is a donation at a certain higher level that requires cultivation and a face-to-face meeting to ask for the gift. That higher-level amount depends on the organization and your community. Major gifts may be given to the annual fund or to a special project. At GLWSM, the amount is $500 and above; at the Abbe Museum, it is $1,000 and above. But the nonprofit down the street from me in Bar Harbor has a much higher major gift threshold. A good rule of thumb is to pick the number that has the most meaning to your organization, and the gift amount should prompt exceptional donor treatment. In other words, our major donors at the Abbe receive more frequent communication from us, and, whenever possible, we set up a special meeting to update them personally about their impact.

STEPS FOR A MAJOR GIFT REQUEST

1. Identify and qualify the prospect. Does the prospect have linkage, interest, and ability?
2. Prepare a brief biography of the individual for the solicitor's reference.
3. Select the lead contact person and the staff person who will accompany. It is always best to go in pairs to make sure the conversation flows smoothly and that the donor is heard correctly (four ears are really better than two).
4. Prepare a written proposal that includes the case for support or the giving opportunity and the amount requested. Keep it brief and to the point.
5. Insert the proposal into a nice folder with marketing materials that may interest the donor (i.e., press clipping from a great kids' event, graphical analysis of budget performance, recent newsletter, images with captions, etc.). Do not miss an opportunity to show the donor how much the museum is loved by the community.
6. Set up the appointment and do not be late! Be very clear about how much time you need when scheduling and stick to your estimate. Be sure to indicate that you are asking for the meeting to share an opportunity with the donor. Make it clear that this is not a social call (one of the solicitors on this visit should know this person and should schedule the meeting).
7. During the meeting, be sure to read the donor's verbal and nonverbal cues. If he is not interested in small talk, do not push it. If small talk is encouraged, be ready with topics to cover. I enjoy asking the donor what her favorite museum experience was and why. Or ask about the last time she visited a museum on vacation. You can also ask about other charities she might have a passion for and why. Just be ready to converse and certainly, if appropriate, find out who she is personally. Do not forget to be human. It is also a good idea to read up on communication styles (DISC, VAK, Social Styles) before your appointment so that you can identify the donor's communication preferences. And smile!
8. Allow for conversation around the organizational mission and the types of programs, exhibits, and collections the museum is responsible for—be sure a bright light is shown on the museum at least briefly during the conversation.

(continued)

9. If this is a donor who has a nice giving record, be sure to share with her the impact of her giving so far.
10. Clearly and plainly ask for the amount you have identified in the proposal.
11. Answer questions honestly. If you do not have the answer, tell the donor you will follow up with the answer as soon as you get back to the office. But there should not be many questions you cannot answer—be prepared.
12. If the answer is yes, be sure to immediately thank the donor and confirm whether she will send a check or would like to be invoiced. And ask her how she would like her name to appear in the newsletter and annual report. If the answer is maybe, then ask her when you may call to follow up. If the answer is no, then ask her when you might check back with her for future opportunities. In this instance, a no is really a maybe. By granting the appointment, the donor is indicating a level of willingness. You just have not hit the right mark yet.
13. Once you return to the office, dash off a handwritten thank-you, no matter what answer she gave.
14. Document the visit in your donor database.

To strategize major gift approaches, in a closed and confidential meeting, the development committee will discuss the names of potential donors in the community and determine how much to ask for and who the best contact person is (i.e., who knows him or her best). Many of the individuals identified will likely be new or existing members and will already have a link with the organization.

There is a skill to making personal asks, and if you are prepared, the nervousness will be less of an issue. Practicing with a board member, colleague, or friend before your first ask will help. See textbox 2.7 for a checklist to use as you prepare and implement a major gift request. The same checklist can be used when you prepare a corporate sponsorship request.

One of the most memorable donations Karen Binder, executive director at Blithewold, recalls is a major gift that secured a horticulture endowment.

Only six years into the founding and saving of the organization from a private developer, a board member and I approached a well-known philanthropist and asked for a $1 million gift. The donor received us and our information, but the decision took several months. A few months later, I was in my office and received a call from the donor's office. I was informed the donor would indeed donate $1 million to our fledging organization. The news literally took my breath away, and I had goose bumps all over my body. I ended the call with profuse thanks and then ran down the hall to tell the director of horticulture. The gift was a transformational moment for our organization as the gift meant our organization's effort, staff and board, and our work generated the confidence and trust of such a well-regarded philanthropist.

With a strong case, passion for your organization, and bravery, you too can have goose bump moments that strengthen your museum and fulfill your mission.

Sponsorships

Sponsorships can support your organization's programs, exhibits, and events; individuals as well as businesses can serve as sponsors by donating to your specific request. In return, the sponsor receives recognition and an association with a particular product the museum delivers. For many businesses, this is valuable advertising.

As stated earlier, only 4 percent of annual contributions are from corporate gifts. This would tell you that you should not spend too much time on securing sponsorships; however, depending on where you are in the United States, sponsorships offer unique marketing opportunities for businesses. In fact, many businesses do not classify their sponsorships as a charitable contribution but rather as a marketing expense. And corporations can be good sources of in-kind support or volunteers. Even if a business declines to write you a check, it can do you a great deal of good by putting your event poster or membership information in its employee lunchroom or newsletter.

Corporate giving can be a sticky wicket. In order to attract a diverse pool of corporate sponsors, you may have to produce high-profile projects or events. But sometimes your local bank, large employer, or supermarket will have an affinity for a special children's program you do each year, and there is value in having a business's name attached. Here again, researching the corporate-giving pattern in your community is the first step in landing sponsorship dollars.

To get started, generate a list of possible business sponsors. If you live in a small town, go ahead and put every business on that list (it may look just like the table in textbox 2.4). Spend time identifying correct mailing addresses and the contact person you need to reach. Many companies will have a corporate-giving representative (sometimes that person is far away at corporate headquarters); others will want you to direct your request to the owner or manager. With your list in place, start carving out fundable projects—exhibits, school programs, free-admission days, family programs—and prepare a budget for each. It is a good idea to attend chamber of commerce meetings and programs to connect with the business community or join a local service club (i.e., Rotary, Kiwanis).

Depending on the project and your fundraising fitness, you can begin seeking sponsors in one of two ways: by direct mail with a follow-up call or in a face-to-face appointment. For example, if you are asking businesses to sponsor a concert series with $100 or $500 gifts, a direct mail piece may do just fine (use the annual fund model for the design of the mailing). But you will need a fairly large mailing list the first time to make sure you get a decent return. For the top ten to twenty prospects on the mailing list, follow up with a call to see if they received the letter and talk with them about the proposal. Be sure to find out if they are going to fund your request before you hang up. And be very willing to invoice them.

For larger sponsorship requests in the neighborhood of $1,000 and above, a face-to-face appointment is required. In the same way you secured and prepared for a major gift request, you will make your case to the owner or manager at his or her place of business; if you can arrange it, also have this person visit your museum and spend some time with you. Never assume that he or she has visited the museum; a business may choose to sponsor you for the advertising exposure and may be less familiar with your mission and how you fulfill it.

It is a good idea to ask a business to become a sponsor only once a year, but some businesses may really like your organization and the association. This may reveal interest in a number of sponsorship opportunities, which you can bundle together into one proposal.

In the end, if you treat the sponsorship development process the same way you do major gifts, you will streamline efforts with the same degree of success. The key difference is that with corporate sponsors, you need to outline in your proposal how you will promote their businesses (i.e., on a donor wall, in print media, on the website, on a special marquee, etc.). Get creative, and think of places where you feel comfortable inserting a corporate logo. Remember, the business owner may be thinking philanthropically when saying yes to a sponsorship, but she is also thinking about how to market her business to the community at large. (See page 92 in chapter 4 in this book for legal issues related to sponsorships.)

Additional Income and Fundraising Strategies

Keeping a diverse and healthy income stream coming into the organization is a goal we all share in the museum community. While this chapter prescribes a kick-start approach to getting fundraising going, you may be attracting dollars in other ways, and they need tending as well. Pay close attention to earned income, fundraising events, the need for a capital or endowment campaign, planned giving, and government support (if applicable).

WHAT IF MY BOARD WON'T FUNDRAISE?

Simply put, if your board refuses to fundraise, you're in a bit of a pickle. But it's not hopeless. The nonprofit sector functions because board members and staff fundraise side by side in their communities, and if you let the board off the hook, the organization is in jeopardy. Here are just a few ways you can help the board become more comfortable with its fundraising role:

1. Recognize that fundraising takes many forms. It's not always a direct, face-to-face ask that is needed from board members, but they all need to find a way to plug into fundraising. Perhaps you're planning a special fundraising event. Have a board-level task force produce the event in total, alleviating the burden on the director.
2. During a board retreat, integrate training. Bring in a local development officer as a guest speaker or schedule a webinar during the retreat.[1] Introduce select readings, and find time for discussion. Be sure you create a continuum of training that both develops the existing board member and educates the new board member.
3. Ask the board to thank people for you. Of course, you will have sent the standard thank-you letter with a personal note, but ask board members to drop a personal note for certain gifts and/or contacts. While this isn't an ask, it is a critical part of the fundraising cycle.
4. Ask for names. As you develop a membership mailing list or other direct mail piece, ask board members to give you a list of names and addresses to include in the mailing. Everyone can do this; there really is no excuse for a board member to refuse to crack open his or her address book or holiday mailing list and share some names. Make it an annual goal for each board member to provide five to ten new names for mailings and have him or her write a personal note on the letter before it goes into the mail.
5. Get yourself and other board members invited to social events. Maybe a board member has an annual Memorial Day picnic. Ask her to invite the board so that members can meet new people and start to broaden the network. Have a board member host an intimate dinner party so that you can get to know his friends casually. As director you're there as a guest, but you also have the chance to learn about interests and build relationships.

(continued)

6. Carry the torch. While the board's fundraising skill set may take longer to develop than you would like, don't stop fundraising. Sometimes the director will have to go the extra mile to secure funds, but the more success and ease of fundraising you share with the board, the more attractive the process becomes. Everyone wants to be part of a winning team, and when you're hitting fundraising goals, you are winning!

Note

1. The dean for advancement at a local college or university would be an excellent speaker.

Earned Income

The most consistent way to earn income is through museum admissions, gift shop sales, program fees, and rentals. A business plan is the best way to strategically develop this area, but as you can imagine, developing a business plan requires an in-depth discussion beyond the scope of this chapter. In short, in a business plan you will share the need and ideas for revenue, identify the market around you and who you want to reach, describe what it will cost to invest in your strategy, offer income and expense projections, outline how you will get the word out (e.g., advertising), and monitor and report the results. You may also decide that all of this information can be included as part of a comprehensive marketing plan as described in chapter 1 in Book 4 of this series, *Reaching and Responding to the Audience*. Sharing this information with your board and seeking its input is a great way to get board members engaged in attracting revenue for the museum. You might convene a revenue task force that can analyze these income streams and local competition, then brainstorm opportunities.

Fundraising Events

Beware the special event designed to raise money for an organization. By the time you calculate staff time, volunteer time, and cash investment for a gala, festival, or other event, you have usually reached astronomical costs in proportion to the annual budget. But if you can create an event that raises a significant amount of money and is meaningful to your community, then it may be worth the risk.

If you have a great idea for an event, and you are not sure how much you can invest to make it a go, try smaller-scale events and measure the results. For example, before we launched the Taste of Montgomery County at GLWSM, we held a series of small concerts two years beforehand and a smattering of related activities. The time came to either take a leap and go big with an event or decide not to do it. If you have some experience leading into this decision, then you are taking a calculated risk that more board members may be more comfortable with. We decided to make the leap at GLWSM, and it resulted in a profitable model that brings new audiences to the museum grounds each year.

Campaigns

Museums basically engage in two types of large-scale fundraising campaigns: capital and endowment. Capital tends to be the less difficult cause to raise money for because it supports extremely tangible items—building renovation, construction or expansion, historic preservation work, storage furniture, office computers, repairs, a new climate control system. Donors really like to see the objects that represent their gift. Endowment campaigns, conversely, present a challenge because giving money to a savings account is far less sexy, even though the income produces highly tangible things (i.e., programs, staff labor, utility costs, etc.).

For both campaign types, if your resources permit, a feasibility study would be wise. Led by an impartial, outside consultant, this study will interview key individuals and community leaders about the importance of the museum, determine their willingness to give, and establish how much money would be given. This will help determine realistic campaign goals.

Once you are ready to launch the campaign, you need to make sure adequate staff time is applied to the project—someone has to stay on top of it and manage the volunteers and staff engaged in the effort. Additionally, you need a strong board with a readiness to participate. Otherwise, the fundraising goal will likely be unmet, and you have a failed campaign on your hands. You will also need to invest resources to produce a printed booklet or brochure that details the purpose of the campaign and the impact it will have.

With resources in place, create a gift chart that tells you how many gifts of a particular size you need and how many qualified donors you need to identify. A breakdown might look like this:

- *Fundraising goal:* $1 million to support operating costs
- *Quiet phase:*
  - two $100,000 gifts
  - six $50,000 gifts
  - ten $25,000 gifts

- *Public phase:*
  - fifteen $10,000 gifts
  - ten $5,000 gifts
  - fifty $1,000 gifts

Gifts that come in may not follow this pattern. Revising the chart will keep the total goal active in everyone's minds.

Large campaigns benefit from a quiet and a public phase. At the outset, the board members decide how much has to be raised quietly, face-to-face in boardrooms and meetings, before issuing a public campaign challenge to realize the total goal. In the above gift chart example, the quiet phase ends once $750,000 in gifts is reached. The public phase will not likely produce as many large gifts as described above; there will be smaller gifts such as $25, $50, and $100, which will add up to the total quickly. One word of caution: It is a rare successful campaign that achieves its total goal without a preexisting donor base.

Planned Giving

There are many options for individuals to direct their wealth during their lifetime and upon their death (i.e., charitable remainder trusts, bequests, etc.). Developing a simple document or brochure that outlines ways people can help you is a good first step.

It is important to remind individuals that your museum is a viable recipient of their generosity and that their legacy will be held in capable hands. You can transmit this information in your newsletters, through a direct mail effort, and via key professionals in your community. For example, trust officers, CPAs, estate-planning attorneys, and wealth managers are often the most likely professionals to have discussions with community members who are actively looking to make a bequest or charitable gift. Make sure these professionals have the museum's information close at hand.

As the organization's finances grow and stabilize, the development committee may designate a planned giving expert, who will cultivate planned gifts within the community, or you may contract with a wealth planner to help guide this process. Whatever you do, make sure that a donor is advised by a financial professional or attorney during the process.

Government Support

Your museum may be city-, county-, or state-owned and funded, and you likely have a nonprofit friends group funding special projects or the operating budget (quasi-governmental). If this describes your budget support, then

TEXTBOX 2.9

FUNDRAISING PLAN OUTLINE

1. *Introduction:* Offer a brief introduction about philanthropy in general and how it is evident locally. A description of the plan's purpose is valuable as well.
2. *Community research:* In this section, share the results of your community assessment and describe who will be involved in development efforts (e.g., development committee). Through research, you will begin to understand both what the community cares about and how community members view your organization, as well as get a sense of your own readiness.
3. *Establishment of a development program:* Now that you understand your community, spend time researching and documenting fundraising strategies. With your research in hand, outline the methods your organization will employ. As a suggested starting point, most museums rely on a membership program for their basic income, and it is the best way for a museum to establish a donor base. Be sure to identify training needs for board members and staff.
4. *Case statement development:* Before leaving the starting gate, you need to articulate the reasons people should give. It needs to be crystal clear why a donor should give and how the money will be used. If you've just completed a strategic plan, you have oodles of information about why the museum matters and where it is headed. A great case statement is made by demonstrating the impact of a donor's gift along with the details of a project. In this section of the plan, articulate the most important reasons people should give, followed by your approach to case statement development.
5. *Annual membership drives:* Establish the time of year and number of mailings for acquiring new members (acquisition mailing). The nature of your membership program can be identified here, including benefits offered and the renewal cycle (frequency and type of mailings). You will need to identify the source(s) of acquisition names (i.e., board members turning in names, exchanging lists with collaborators, purchasing a list, etc.). Renewal mailing frequency should be established as well, preferably on a monthly basis and on the anniversary of a member's last renewal.[1]

(continued)

6. *Annual fund:* Once the membership program is established, determining the timing of your first annual fund mailing is next. To alleviate donor confusion, it is best to make sure the membership program has taken root (after one to two renewal cycles) before asking for donations above the membership level. It is also advisable to segment your mailing list so that you're not sending a membership renewal letter and an annual appeal letter to the same house at the same time.

7. *Major gifts program:* With a well-established annual fund appeal process, you can start identifying prospects for major gifts. How you define a major gift depends on your museum ($500 and above? $1,000 and above? $2,500 and above?). In this section you may also describe your approach to donor-prospect research (e.g., paying for database access, relying on your own database, sharing information among board members, etc.).

8. *Retention:* Intrinsic to the fundraising process is the expression of gratitude. The number and type of thank-you letters should be identified here, as should the signatory. Another way to keep members and donors close is to host annual events or parties to show your gratitude, in addition to giving standard museum discounts.

9. *Grant development:* Identify the frequency and annual goals of grant-writing projects, keeping in mind the balance between your time and the amount of money requested. It is helpful to back up this section with a spreadsheet that identifies likely and past grant makers matched to specific projects, listed with deadlines. As chapter 3 of this book shows, board members and community members often believe that getting a grant is simple and will solve everything. Demonstrating a strategy around grant writing in your fundraising plan will help balance the trustee perspective.

10. *Capital campaign:* Capital campaigns can be time-consuming and costly, but they tend to be easier to conduct. They represent tangible results (i.e., restoration project, expansion wing, etc.). However, board members and staff always know that steady funding is needed for operating expenses and is more difficult to secure. With an established membership and annual funding campaign, adding a capital campaign to the mix should impact operating income minimally. The key is proper timing, an established donor base, and suitable prospect research—you have to ask the right people

at the right time. If you have a capital campaign on the horizon, identify it here and identify your timeline.

11. *Endowment campaign:* The proper timing for an endowment campaign is contingent upon a capital campaign's timing and success. For an endowment campaign, a feasibility study is essential, and its timing can be identified here.

12. *Fundraising events:* Identify each year's planned events and the goals for each. This can include a major fundraising event as well as small cultivation parties. It is easy to fall into the special event trap, where board members are comfortable throwing an event together, but its development goals are an afterthought. Special events are the mother of all time eaters for museum staff—if there is no logical, clear reason for the event, do not hold it.

13. *Planned giving:* This section can identify how information about your organization can be disseminated to wealth planners and attorneys—an easily overlooked piece of fundraising. Most small museums do not have a planned giving expert on staff, but they can connect with knowledgeable people in the community. This section can also identify what steps will be taken upon notification of a bequest, charitable trust gift, and the like.

14. *Earned income:* While earned income is not typically within the purview of the development committee, in small museums, it helps to consolidate information on all income streams into one plan. Identify for the board how the organization generates earned income (e.g., admissions, gift shop sales, rentals, etc.) and any strategies you have for increasing income in this area. You may want to create a task force to develop out-of-the-box thinking; if you have certain earned income goals for the future, a separate plan could develop out of this fundraising plan (i.e., a business or marketing plan).

15. *Government support:* As with earned income, government support is not the development committee's focus, but it should be on the board's radar. If your organization receives annual government support, it is critical to tend to this funding source. Government support can wax and wane with political winds, and it is *never* safe to assume that financial support in one budget cycle will continue to the next. Strategies for reporting back to government leaders and other communication strategies should be outlined here. In some cases, formalizing support through a written agreement will prevent surprises.

(continued)

TEXTBOX 2.9 *(Continued)*

16. *Evaluation:* The most obvious determinant of the plan's success is an increase in donations and an improvement in the organization's bottom line. It can also be measured through anecdotal examples and surveys. This information should be regularly reported in board meetings and communicated to the community through newsletters and press releases. In addition, if funds are not flowing in as projected, course corrections are needed. How you plan to evaluate your fundraising progress should be spelled out here.

Note

1. Fundraising professionals debate about the frequency of renewal mailings. I have always preferred a monthly schedule because it keeps you plugged into fundraising in a systematic fashion, plus it promotes cash flow. At my current organization, we send renewals more on a quarterly schedule because we're a seasonal organization. Mailings are timed with our operational patterns. Whatever renewal cycle you choose, it should definitely be more frequent than once or twice a year.

it would be wise to enact safeguards to protect funding levels. Through recent years, public funds for museums have dwindled significantly, leaving a funding void that jeopardizes the important work museums do. Before you arrive at budget season, you can do a few things to improve your odds for continued funding or budget increases.

During the months between budget months, spend quality time with your elected officials—talking about the museum, showing them around the facility, sending event invitations, providing written status updates—and help them become informed leaders. When they enter the budget cycle, there should be no question about the importance of your museum to the community.

While very little can be done if political leaders decide to defund your organization, you can control the timing a bit. Working with an attorney, draft a formal agreement that determines the fiduciary responsibilities of the nonprofit friends group and the governmental agency. The agreement should identify how much notice each party requires, should there be funding cuts (e.g., ninety days, six months). It should also describe how each entity funds the organization, who is responsible for governance,[7] and who has signatory authority over any future agreements or addenda. Through proactive conversations and formal agreements, government support can become less uncertain.

Measuring Progress

The most obvious determinant of how your fundraising efforts are doing is an increase in donations and an improvement in the organization's bottom line. It can also be measured through anecdotal examples and surveys—how do people feel about giving to your museum?

To keep the board members informed and energized, this information should be regularly reported in board meetings and communicated to the community through the newsletter and press releases. In addition, if funds are not flowing in as projected, course corrections are needed. Finding yourself deep into a new initiative and learning that you do not have the funds to complete the task will not only imperil your initiative but promote negative feelings about management and affect board morale. And heaven forbid the information gets out into the community—your donors might start questioning whether a gift to your museum is a good investment.

Remember, fundraising is about sharing a story. And who better to tell the story than the staff members who take great care of the museum and the board members who volunteer their time and expertise in service. If you believe in what you are doing, it is easy to make the next person believe too. Being strategic about who that next person might be is the secret to fundraising. Now, get out there and fundraise!

Special Thanks

Special thanks to Ron Newlin and Stacy Klingler for their thoughtful critique and to Karen Binder and Tim Garrity for their excellent institutional examples.

Recommended Resources

Brophy, Sarah. *Is Your Museum Grant-Ready? Assessing Your Organization's Potential for Funding*. Lanham, MD: AltaMira Press. 2005.

Center for Nonprofit Excellence (CNE). "Nonprofit Business Plan Outline," CNE, www .cfnpe.org/ResourcesTools/NonprofitBusinessPlanOutline/tabid/169/Default.aspx.

Eisenstein, Amy M. *50 Asks in 50 Weeks: A Guide to Better Fundraising for Your Small Development Shop*. Rancho Santa Margarita, CA: Charity Channel Press, 2010.

Ellis, Susan J. *The Volunteer Recruitment (and Membership Development) Handbook*. Philadelphia: Energize, Inc., 2002.

Flanagan, Joan. *Successful Fundraising: A Complete Handbook for Volunteers and Professionals*. 2nd ed. New York: McGraw-Hill, 2002.

Panas, Jerold. *Asking: A 59-Minute Guide to Everything Board Members, Volunteers, and Staff Must Know to Secure the Gift*. Medfield, MA: Emerson and Church, 2006–2007.

Prince, Russ Alan, and Karen Maru File. *The Seven Faces of Philanthropy: A New Approach to Cultivating Major Donors.* San Francisco: Jossey-Bass, 2001.

Schaff, Terry, and Doug Schaff. *The Fundraising Planner: Working Model for Raising the Dollars You Need.* San Francisco: Jossey-Bass, 1999.

Schumacher, Edward. *Building Your Endowment.* San Francisco: Jossey-Bass, 2003.

Taylor, Martha A., and Sondra Shaw-Hardy, ed., *The Transformative Power of Women's Philanthropy.* San Francisco: Jossey-Bass, 2006.

Warwrick, Mal. *The Mercifully Brief, Real-World Guide to Raising $1,000 Gifts by Mail.* Medfield, MA: Emerson and Church, 2005.

Notes

1. "Giving USA 2010: The Annual Report on Philanthropy for 2009," Pursuant, www.pursuantmedia.com/givingusa/0510/export/GivingUSA_2010_ExecSummary_Print.pdf (accessed June 8, 2011).

2. Pursuant, "The Annual Report on Philanthropy for 2009."

3. There are over 1.5 million registered nonprofits in the United States. See "Quick Facts about Nonprofits," National Center for Charitable Statistics, http://nccs.urban.org/statistics/quickfacts.cfm.

4. Where I work now, the Abbe Museum in Bar Harbor, Maine, membership fees begin at $40. This difference reflects local trends and the community's capacity and philanthropic culture.

5. If you have a gift shop with big-ticket items for sale, you might offer a free membership with a certain sale price. At the Abbe Museum Shop, we sell high-priced basketry and other Native arts. Previously, each time an unknown high-end buyer walked out the door, we were missing a cultivation opportunity. Now, with a purchase of $500 or more, the buyer receives a free membership.

6. If you have a fearless volunteer who is willing to make the pitch, that is all the better. It need not be the director every time, but it has to be someone who can communicate a passion for the organization.

7. At GLWSM, in the agreement, the city of Crawfordsville, Indiana, gave the governance role to our friends group, the Lew Wallace Study Preservation Society, and the relationship is described in the agreement. The society governs on behalf of the owner, the city.

CHAPTER THREE

"OH, JUST WRITE A GRANT AND FIX THE BUILDING": LANDING GRANTS TO SUPPORT YOUR INSTITUTION

Benjamin Hruska

After earning my master's degree in public history from Wichita State University at the end of 2004, I accepted a position at a site I now describe as the smallest museum, on the smallest island, in the smallest state. During the early winter months of 2005, I disembarked from the ferry that takes one to Block Island, Rhode Island, and began my work as director of the Block Island Historical Society (BIHS). Founded 1942, the organization was chartered to protect the material and cultural heritage of this island community first settled by Europeans in 1661. As the society's only full-time employee, I knew I needed financial help outside of our membership in order to move the organization in a new direction.

During my first week on the island, I sat in a barber's chair facing the society's 130-year-old building and noticed it was looking a little worse for wear. As we discussed the condition of the building and the organization, the barber stated, "Oh, just write a grant and fix the building." However, like many small museums, BIHS needed help on a number of levels. What should be the initial focus? Should I apply for a grant for the exterior of the building to improve its physical look? Should we consider seeking a grant aimed at organizing our collection of objects and archives? Or would the most beneficial step involve writing a grant proposal to treat the building and wooden objects for the powderpost beetles that infested portions of the building? Over the coming months and years, we placed these priorities in order and earned grants that greatly improved our position in the community, as well as the state of our building and the collections it houses.

In the small museum environment, we are constantly doing more with less in comparison to our larger sister organizations. However, besides money, archival boxes, and exhibit space, our most lacking resource is time. There is precious little time not only to maintain our established exhibitions and programs but also to devote to new ventures. Obtaining grants provides the avenue to move into new territory for your small organizations. However, it is a serious and time-consuming enterprise and is more difficult than simply "writing a grant." Utilizing your limited hours for the investigating, researching, and writing of specific

Photo 3.1. The Block Island Historical Society's museum building, located on Block Island, Rhode Island (taken in the summer of 2010 while undergoing the fourth and final phase of the complete restoration of the historic structure, originally constructed as a seasonal hotel in the early 1870s). This restoration's first phase was initiated with a successful grant from the Rhode Island Historical Preservation and Heritage Commission in the fall of 2007.

targeted grants holds the potential for increasing your organization's footprint on the community. This short chapter aims to provide a roadmap for obtaining grants with the limited time available to those of us in the small museum world.

The Basics

Starting with You

A critical step required before considering possible sources of funding from grants is to take a true "gut check" of your institution. Understanding success in the nonprofit world of small museums is considerably different than in for-profit enterprises. As Jim Collins writes in *Good to Great and the Social Sectors*, in small organizations such as ours, "money is only an input, and not a measure of greatness."[1] This gut check of the organization includes all aspects of your institution from the board of directors, administration, staff, and volunteers to members of and visitors to your organization. Questions to ask of these stakeholders could include the following: Is our mission clearly defined? Where do weaknesses exist in our operation? Where are we falling short in regard to reaching our goals? How does our audience view our daily operation and overall success or failure in meeting our defined mission?

Once compiled, the answers to these tough questions will allow your organization to define what its peak success would look like. This peak success will not be obtained with one exhibition, one educational program, or the awarding of a single grant. However, understanding and, most importantly, articulating this long-range goal will aid in the successful securing of grants. This process will allow for a clearer understanding of your organization's short- and long-term needs. It will help identify your current audience and areas where expanding your audience is possible. The process will clarify how your organization is unique in its operations in comparison with other small museums in your immediate area. And lastly, it will afford you an honest assessment of the quality of your organization's activities. These answers will give you a clearer understanding of your organization's strengths and weaknesses and prove beneficial in moving it forward as well as assist you in finding partners to aid in this transition toward a new direction.[2]

Who Gives and How

One major component of the research phase is deciphering which agencies award grants. These groups (and some individuals) are numerous, and many award multiple grants per year. On the governmental level, research grants are appropriated by the federal, state, and even municipal levels. Private funding is more diverse, with possibilities including community groups, volunteer agencies, private individuals, and foundations. For small museums, private, corporate, and community foundations provide a good source of grant awards.[3]

Just as we need to reinforce the amount of research time required in implementing a solid program in the successful obtaining of grants, we also need to understand the many avenues used for the distribution of funds. These can include grants aimed at capital funds, examples of which include additions or restorations of a building or a major purchase for the museum, including computer systems. A second possible form provides funds to increase or even start an endowment, which is aimed at producing funds for operating expenses. Grants are also very diverse in the issuing of funds. Paid out in a number of ways, these funds may come out over a number of years, all at once, or on a performance basis.[4] While you will learn the specific details of who gives and how more fully once your grant process moves forward, it is important to know the range of ways in which funds are acquired so that you cast as wide a net as possible for future funding in reaching your organization's long-term goals.

Who Wins

Grants from foundations represent the largest pool of possible grant funding, and understanding who is successful in obtaining grants of $10,000 or more gives us an idea of who is winning. The *Boston Globe* reported that in 2001 over 26 percent of large foundation grants went to universities or colleges. Organizations classified as "arts, performing arts, and humanities groups" earned just fewer than 6 percent of these large awarded grants. The two classifications representing the very bottom end were environmental nonprofits and groups devoted to promoting civil rights.[5] What are the universities and colleges doing that is allowing for such dominance in receiving grants from foundations? More importantly, what can small museums learn from the tactics employed by these successful universities?

Key to Success: The Relationship

Chances are that as a small museum, you are not trying to compete with funding raised by the local university. However, understanding how these massive grants are acquired holds the potential for success for small museums. The key to the university model is perfecting the relationship with the foundation. The director of foundation fundraising at Columbia University, Michael Rodin, calls this method "total relationship management."[6] This concept involves devoting entire staffs of these organizations to cultivating, maintaining, and harvesting relationships with large donors. Large amounts of time devoted by university staff result in huge successes. This investment of time allows possible donors to know not only of the university's need but also about how their funding will be utilized and what benefits will result from their gift. As H. Peter Karoff of the Philanthropic Initiative points out, donors think, "I know how to give $100 million to my college. I don't know how to give $100 million to help kids in the inner city."[7] Now, chances are, your organization is not looking for a $100 million donor, and you may wonder why this quote was included in this chapter. The reason is that these donors know how to give to a college not only because of name recognition but because they know someone, and, more importantly, trust someone, at this institution. People give to people, not to organizations. Understanding this helps us realize small museums hold a real advantage in going after donors and foundations due to our smallness since we are normally run by a core group of staff and board members. Getting your museum personnel out of the museum and into contact with these possible donors, large or small, is the next step. While universities have their alumni to communicate their mission and need, those of us in small museums do not have this initial advantage. However, proper use of our staffs, boards of directors, and members' collective contacts moves us in that same direction.

Identifying and Developing Relationships

In identifying support for possible grants, begin with sources with whom your museum personnel are acquainted. Even the smallest organization most likely has a network it may not even consider as a helpful start in forming a network. Board members, staff, and volunteers all have friends with similar interests. Almost all these interests or hobbies involve fundraising on some level, be it an American Legion Auxiliary bake sale or chili fundraiser to send the local high school to march in the Rose Bowl parade. In this opening phase of identifying help, do not fear casting your net too wide. Any contact you can harvest in terms of grant writing or fundraising is a source of possible help. As we all know, many individuals involved in volunteer organizations are involved in multiple entities aimed at improving their communities. With this in mind, add any organization or personal contacts to this initial listing of possible supporters in not only targeting grants but also providing advice during the grant process.[8]

The second phase is simply to research possible grant sources. Who in the past, even the very distant past, has given to your organization? To whom have these past supporters given funds recently? Contact small museums similar to your organization in scope, size, and mission for possible success stories. Even these small organizations well outside your immediate area possess information for successfully developing relationships with donors. Look for donors who are funding organizations similar to your small museum. Investigate the possibility of these organizations funding a grant in your area. Also look for similar foundations or donors in your area that have not previously given to small museums. If they have not, the chances are they are not currently in a relationship with a small museum. Enter you and your organization.[9]

Once this list of individuals, foundations, and agencies is compiled, you need to establish connections and then work at staying connected. As with all relationships, developing relationships with these organizations, individuals, and groups will take time. To begin, their names need to be added to all your forms of outreach, from mailing lists to all the electronic forms you utilize for updating your membership and friends. Over a period of months, this process will demonstrate the impact of your small museum on your community through your sponsored events and other outreach activities. A special event can also be held for these potential grantors in demonstrating your past activities, future goals, and ways they can join your team in reaching these goals. All these steps, or some modifications of them, represent aspects of the "total relationship management" that places universities on the top of the heap in gathering large grants. Structuring their tactics to fit your small museum will yield dividends in reaching your long-term goals.[10]

Defining Goals

Now that your organization is developing and maintaining relationships, the time has arrived to define your specific goals and the difficult task of prioritizing the essential steps toward achieving them. This very well can prove the most difficult, as board members, administration, and staff may not agree on the minute details of the final goal. While this may be a painful step, accomplishing it will yield results once the grant writing begins, as it will allow your organization to move ahead with a single-minded purpose. Concrete sample statements of the single-minded purpose include "We are seeking funding to rehabilitate our historic building" and "We are seeking funding to digitally catalog our collection of objects." With an agreed-on plan of action in which goals are clear and focused, the range of possible grants is narrowed to those that best match these goals, allowing for focus in the months ahead.[11]

Research Tools in Finding and Exploring Grants

The world of grants is similar to that of cheese. On the surface, one could ask, "How many kinds of cheese are there?" The original estimate of a number that you could count on one hand expands rapidly on examination. Grants, like types of cheese, are diverse in flavor and texture. Investigating the diverse range of grants, including those outside the realm of small museums, can provide information on the depth of the grant well. A quick examination of grant Web pages can give you and your grant-writing team food for thought.

- "Example Grant Applications," Florida Division of Cultural Affairs (www.florida-arts.org/grants/GrantExamples.htm)
- "Grant Applicants, Grant Reviewers, Grant Recipients," Institute of Museum and Library Services (www.imls.gov)
- "Federal Grants," Nonprofit Expert (www.nonprofitexpert.com/federal_grants.htm)
- "USDA National Agricultural Library Rural Information Center," U.S. Department of Agriculture (www.nal.usda.gov/ric/ricpubs/fundguide.html)

Understanding Costs Involved

Once the overarching goals are agreed upon, the organization needs to understand the costs of pursuing and earning grants. We know that understanding the organizational gut check and relationship building takes time. However, before further pursuing grant proposals, all stakeholders need to realize the time involved. This is not to discourage your staff or board members from the action of going after grants. However, the hours needed in researching, drafting, and editing grants are many. Likewise, ethically completing grants, staying in communication with the grant maker, and putting in the man-hours to direct extra resources and/or personnel from the grant funds can also represent significant tasks. Fully understanding this will help all on board realize that grant writing is a long-term process and will aid you in considering the scale of your proposal and goal for the grant.[12]

My experience working with our team at the BIHS included taking three years to hook the big grant. This three-year period included rejections of grant applications, successful awarding of smaller grants, and getting to know each of our team members' strengths and weaknesses. Like any team in a sporting event, our grant-writing team learned the best ways to work with each other in taking on the large grant. This process took a great deal of time and effort. However, for those organizations willing to devote the amount of required time, landing the large grant can serve as a steppingstone in launching the organization in a new and exciting direction.

Ethical Concerns

Obtaining and implementing grants, like all matters in your organization, includes ethical considerations. The American Association for State and Local History's Statement of Professional Standards and Ethics highlights a number of ethical aspects in the small museum realm, including use of historical resources, interpretation, and management, which covers areas touching grant-related activities. The bedrock of your organization's moxie, especially with relationship building, is public trust. Not fulfilling a grant or not conducting your organization in an ethical manner while completing a grant endangers that public trust. Also, your organization needs to understand that, in many instances, receiving a grant is a legally binding contract between you and the grant maker. Required steps in completing a grant are numerous and may possibly include finding matching funds, providing detailed reporting of the project, including documentation, and setting a date for the completion of the project. All these considerations and, more importantly, the time and energy involved must be fully understood before your organization takes on this legal and ethical responsibility.[13]

The Grant

After creating your pool of possible supporters and understanding the effort involved in the first stages of considering a grant, its time to dive into the grant-proposal process itself. Your efforts so far have given you a selection of the most conducive foundations or grant makers in relation to your organization's goals.

This is the point for making direct contact with the possible supporter and expressing your organization's intent to apply for the specific award. Ask not only for advice on how to succeed or giving trends over the past few years but also for the specific requirements for all material needed for the grant. Many may have the ability to send their guidelines in the form of what is termed a request for proposal.[14]

Drafting

Implementing the drafting of the first grant proposal may take many forms. However, all sources strongly encourage some form of teamwork. Depending on your organization's strengths, you may have multiple authors or editors. However, having too many folks involved also represents a danger in slowing down the process. A team made up of fewer than five members is recommended for most grants. Whatever your method, involving more than just one pair of eyes will produce a better proposal in the end. However, below are a few things that cannot be overlooked. Some of these points may seem minor, but failure to follow them may account for why one out of every two very great proposals is not accepted.[15]

- Target the proposal to fit the grant maker or foundation's mission statement.
- Clearly state the reason for the proposed funding and how it would aid your stated need.
- In writing and editing, remind yourself to use economy of expression to say the most with the smallest amount of text. Most of these proposals will have a word limit, requiring excellent writing skills.
- Lastly, have someone unfamiliar with your organization read the draft proposal. After reading, this independent reader should be able to answer the following questions: What is the mission of this small museum? How would the grant help? How would the funds be utilized?

These basic key factors should be considered in the first drafting of the proposal to avoid problems in the final proposal.[16]

Components of the Grant

Grant components will vary in the minor details. Depending on the purpose and organization applied to, these may include proposed exhibit texts, images, or resumes of staff or board members. However, most will require the following in some form:

- *Abstract:* This concise summary of the proposal is normally under two hundred words.
- *Statement of need:* This clearly written prose quickly sums up your organization's shortfall and how addressing it will benefit your small museum.
- *Goals:* This section states your museum's goals and how this particular grant will aid in meeting them. It is important to describe this quantitatively, which allows for measureable progress in reporting back to the grant maker.
- *Methodology:* This section demonstrates your method for employing the grant funding and addressing the stated need.
- *Budget:* Quite possibly the most important and certainly the most time-consuming section of most proposals, this section will include detailed information on the spending of the funds if the grant is awarded, including raw materials, staff times, in-kind promised services, and volunteer hours. The adage "The devil is in the details" applies here. Securing the services of a number of individuals with experience in working with detailed budgets is a must.[17]

Time Management in Writing

Thus far, we understand the components of the average grant and the keys to success in fundraising for organizations like large universities with huge staffs and budgets devoted solely to gathering money. Now comes the time to translate this information to the small museum. We lack no other asset more than time. We do not have the luxury of countless staff hours aimed at securing the next grant. To compete with these successful grant-grabbing organizations, we need to do what we do best: get by on less than our larger sister museums. Thus, we must combine our skill set of producing more with less with time management and grant writing.

Placing successful grants in the same realm as your final algebra exam, cramming will not get you the grade you are seeking. And in the business of grants, earning a gentleman's C will not result in the awarding of a grant. So, as when aiming to pass an exam with flying colors, we must begin the process of grant writing just like we started our grant research and relationship building—months and not days ahead of time. Also, starting the drafting and rewriting process weeks ahead of the due date will allow us to better utilize the limited hours of our personnel, be they board members, administrators, staff, or volunteers.

An additional reason for allowing ample time for writing is the number of staff working on the individual portions of the grant. This is especially true in the case of a larger grant, which may cover more than one of the traditional areas of the museum world. For example, a possible grant application may not only ask for an addition to the museum building but also address the exhibition space inside the proposed addition. This proposal would require jargon from a number of fields; therefore, the more time you have to blend the writing into a clear and concise piece, the better the application will be. The weeks of drafting and working on the budget will yield a winning project. One team of authors summed up the solid grant application from the perspective of the grant maker: "Regardless of the source of their funding, all grant-making entities want to help underwrite successful programs that have significant effects."[18] Successful management of your shortage of man-hours over a long period will aid in crafting an application that shows need, plan of action, and the benefits of the implemented plan.

The Heavy Weight: Writing for Foundations

The earning of a grant from a foundation can produce a massive influx of capital for reaching your organization's goals. However, one irony related to large grants from foundations is the extremely limited space your organization has to make its case—often just one to two pages of text. This is a balancing act. You need to cover the bases to show you are ready to fulfill the possible award and also explain your organization's current situation and future goals. This charged task is never easy, so plan on writing multiple drafts to pack in as much needed information as possible. Below is a framework for consideration. Using this skeleton, you can tailor the text to your organization and the foundation you are seeking funding from:

- Your organization's purpose and reason for selecting this particular foundation
- If awarded the grant, the expected outcome for your organization
- How your organization's current status demonstrates its preparedness to fulfill the awarding of a grant from this foundation
- The time line for implementing and completing the grant, if awarded[19]

The portions are not set in stone. Your narrative will need transformation to make the best possible case for your organization in an extremely limited space. Overall, however, remember economy of expression in the end product in grant writing, especially with submissions to foundations. While your text is limited in page length, do not forget the need for a detailed budget for the project. A foundation may ask for this in the initial application package or later in the selection process. If the latter is the case, your organization will look extremely prepared when the needed figures are already completed, demonstrating your organization's seriousness in moving forward.

Submission

Now that several drafts have produced a final application free of spelling, grammar, or budgetary problems, it is time for submission. Most grants include a date by which the application must be postmarked for consideration. One additional way to make your organization's application stand out is to send it in early, demonstrating your seriousness and also management ability. Your application will stand out from the majority of applications submitted on the very last day. Additionally, if the grant maker is in the immediate area, personal delivery will not only show your professionalism but also put a face to your organization. This represents just one more step in your relationship-building campaign. Keep in mind that it is much easier to say no to someone you have never met than to someone with whom you have nurtured even a minor relationship.

Waiting and Perspective

Once the application is submitted, the difficult waiting game begins. However, during this process you must keep your perspective focused on your long-range goals and not just on this one grant. As Jim Collins writes, "In building a great institution, there is no single defining action, no grand program, no one killer innovation, no solitary lucky break, no miracle moment."[20] Your long-range goals, identified during your organizational gut check, travel beyond just one award, exhibit, or grant. Collins, in *Good to Great and the Social Sectors*, uses the analogy of a flywheel on a combustion engine. This device enables continued inertia for the engine to run, but it may take a great deal of energy to get the flywheel up to speed. Once in motion, however, it continues to push energy onward. This is the aim of your organization, to generate energy like a wave pushing you forward toward your goals. Remember that it is easy to support a winner; therefore, it may take a number of tries to capture the first grant. However, once you do, you are well on your way to earning larger and more complex grants in the future.[21]

Dealing with Disappointment

Learning the finer points of grant writing is very much like most sporting activities: Practicing the activity improves your ability. Receiving notification of an unsuccessful grant application should not be looked upon as failure. No matter the result, you gained valuable knowledge relating to all the aspects of the application process. Also, after allowing some time to pass once informed of your unsuccessful attempt, it is helpful to ask the grant-making entity for feedback on your application. What could have improved it overall? Was there a specific problem and, if so, in which portion and how large an issue was it? Gathering this precious feedback is critical in understanding ways to improve future grant proposals. Lastly, be sure an official thank-you is issued to the grant maker. This entity took the time to consider your application and, in some cases, will have provided valuable feedback, so it deserves recognition.

All these tactics were employed at the BIHS in dealing with our first disappointment. However, in requesting feedback, we learned of a number of ways to improve our application. With revisions and more study on grants in this particular aspect of building renovations, we received a successful reply the next year. Details of this experience will follow later in this chapter.

Success

With relationship building, hard work, and team effort, successful notification of a grant award will arrive. Again, an official thank-you needs delivery to the grant maker. Also, information on the grant-awarding process from the grant maker should arrive. However, if it does not within a few days of notification of success, you may request this information. A quick celebration is in order for all who aided in taking this important first step toward achieving your organization's long-term goals. Enjoy the time of celebration, for in the days ahead, you may feel a bit overwhelmed. As the old saying asks, "What does the dog do once he catches the car he has been chasing?"

Success Stories and Real-World Small Museum Examples

Block Island Historical Society

Founded in 1942, the BIHS's mission is to preserve and protect Block Island's material and cultural history. The organization is housed in a three-story Victorian hotel on this sixteen-square-mile island with just under a thousand full-time residents. The museum portion of the building has limited public access during the summer season and on weekends in the early spring and fall months. The collection of objects includes farming and fishing implements, while archival material centers on the sixteen founding families who landed on the island in 1661. The twelve-member board meets three times a year, including the annual meeting held over Labor Day weekend.

In the spring of 2007, three of the society's board members and I formed a team to locate, research, and draft a major grant. First, we considered our organization's greatest need. In 2006 we initiated an ambitious accessioning project for our archives and objects and also launched an oral history project with older island residents, so our collections and community outreach were moving in a progressive direction.

With this in mind, we asked what the greatest hindrance to our organization was in the eyes of the community. The answer was the condition of our historic, three-story, mansard-roofed building, initially constructed as a hotel in the late 1870s. While our organization's community footprint had increased in the previous year, the fact remained that the building's neglected look reinforced the community's notion that the organization was delinquent in its operations. Even though we are located in a resort area where our doors are closed for eight months of the year, our building serves as our billboard to the year-round community for twelve months a year, and its condition needed addressing before we could move forward with our long-term goals.

In looking for possible sources of help, we examined organizations in the immediate area that had experienced success in the past in obtaining grants for their buildings. We did not have to look far, as the island has two historic lighthouses that had taken huge steps in the preservation of their structures. In fact, three BIHS board members also served on the board of one of the lighthouses that had experienced considerable success in obtaining grants during the past decade. In examining the sources of their successes, we zeroed in on one group in particular, the Rhode Island Historical Preservation and Heritage Commission (RIHPHC), whose mission statement coincided with the preservation of our building. This organization is a state-based agency aimed at providing funding for historic preservation and heritage projects. The commission's past winners include a range of sites, including individual structures, archaeological sites, and historic districts.[22] In 2006, the RIHPHC awarded the Southeast Lighthouse Foundation on the island a $100,000 grant that required a matching $100,000 to aid in the completion of the restoration of this structure synonymous with coastal Rhode Island. We also considered other success stories of organizations throughout the state that were awarded RIHPHC funding. Then, we began considering our specific proposal and our initial drafting of the grant.

In the development of our relationship with the RIHPHC, we utilized a multifaceted approach. Since a number of our board members had experienced success with the RIHPHC while working with the Southeast Lighthouse Foundation, they informed their past contacts with the RIHPHC of the BIHS's interest in applying for the 2007 round of grants. Also, I, as acting administrator, and the vice president of the board attended the annual RIHPHC preservation conference. This not only allowed us once again to express our interest personally with the commission's staff but also gave us a chance to visit with past winners of grants from across the state at the annual conference.

While drafting the grant, we divided the workload by focusing on our individual strengths. The three board members with past experience writing successful grants served as the primary authors. As the only full-time employee, I worked at the physical building gathering estimates from local contractors for our building grant. These included estimates for the proposed building restoration, such as the shoring up of the wooden foundation under the building, rehabbing the original wooden gutters, and replacing the mansard roof shingles. This required not only the estimates but also photographs to document the current state of the areas of the building addressed in the grant. Lastly, our budget proposal for the project was compiled by the entire team, led by the treasurer of the board.

After multiple drafts were completed, the time came for submission. We decided to deliver the application personally, and I submitted it in July 2007 to the commission's Providence office. This once again allowed me to see and thank those at the RIHPHC who had worked with us over the preceding weeks in the answering of questions related to the application. The selection process did take some time, but we learned of our successful $50,000 application during the closing months of 2007. This represented a massive step for us, considering we had one full-time staff member and an annual budget under $70,000. While this was a success story, our hopes were somewhat dampened by the sobering news of state budget cuts with the economic downturn, which hit the state of Rhode Island especially hard.

Regardless of the uncertainty, we continued on with our goal of improving the outreach of our society overall. This earned us the Regional Tourism Award from the governor of Rhode Island in May 2008. Shortly thereafter, we learned of the successful funding of the RIHPHC by the state legislature. Work started on our historic building after the 2008 summer season came to a close. While the logistics of any restoration are complicated, the fact that our building is located on an island thirteen miles out to sea added to the complexity. As I write this in early 2010, nearly all goals of the grant have been completed. This includes the reshingling of the mansard roof, the shoring up of the wooden foundation under the building, and new electrical wiring. All these steps have drastically improved the exterior of the building and, combined with our cataloging work with our collections, complements our expanded community outreach.

Logan Museum of Anthropology

Founded in 1893, the Logan Museum of Anthropology has served as an important aspect of Beloit College in Beloit, Wisconsin. With a diverse collection of 175,000 objects from cultures across the world, the Logan Museum has proved an effective partner in the college's museum studies program.[23] While the museum has no direct board, the director reports to a chain of command that includes the dean of academic affairs, the university president, and the board of the university. The staff of the Logan Museum collaborated on the writing, receiving, and implementing of a $350,000 grant from the National Endowment for the Humanities (NEH). This grant, aimed at improving accessibility to the collection, called for careful planning during all stages, from research to consulting with other organizations to writing the grant.[24] Like all successful detailed plans in non- and for-profit organizations, this success did not come about easily.

The Logan success story started with an honest self-assessment in the form of participation in the Conservation Assessment Program from Heritage Preservation. Completed in 2002, this final report provided a detailed preservation plan committed to the care of the anthropology collection and included both short- and long-term goals. The long-term goals included increasing accessibility to the collection by improving the storage of current objects to provide space for future objects.[25] One possible source of support for this long-range goal was the NEH, which is an independent grant-awarding agency of the U.S.

Photo 3.2. The Logan Museum of Anthropology at Beloit College, in Beloit, Wisconsin.

government. The NEH awards grants in the hundreds of thousands of dollars. Winning such a large award required a massive amount of time for researching and drafting the grant proposal.

The curator of collections, Nicolette Meister, completed the research related to the project. First, she conducted a literature review of articles and books related to similar efforts in initiating a massive collections project. Second, other organizations that had recently completed large collections-based programs were consulted on their past successes and failures. Third, the facilities of three newly renovated storage areas were personally visited, allowing for close inspection of new storage systems. Lastly, a pilot project, using a very small percentage of the Logan collection, allowed for testing of the devised methodology for the grant. All four of these research components, including a literature review, conversations with other organizations, personal visits to new museum storage areas, and a pilot project, provided detailed information that proved invaluable when putting together the NEH grant application.[26]

The overall goal stated in the NEH grant proposal was the proper removal of the collection from the storage area, the installation of new storage

Photo 3.3. Ethnology storage before the implementation of the grant.

facilities, and the return of the collection to the original space. Four benefits from this action included "replacing inappropriate and substandard storage equipment," "mitigating inappropriate environmental conditions," "alleviating overcrowding and lack of accessibility," and "creating new space for the growth of collections."[27] The NEH grant proposal called for detailed information on how these four aspects of the project would be completed, which the research conducted beforehand provided. Questions that needed addressing proved extensive. How would artifacts be transported and in what? Where would storage of the collection occur during the process of renovation? What steps would be taken to ensure the collection's safety from breakage or theft? How would all these steps be documented? Effectively addressing these questions required substantial research.[28]

Nicolette Meister, having conducted the majority of the research, drafted the majority of the text. However, her director, Dr. William Green, drafted the text related to the importance of the collection and the Logan Museum's importance in relation to the humanities. This stated much more than "we have old stuff and we need help." This statement placed the collection—and, equally as important, efficient access to it—into the larger framework of the humanities on the national level. Once Meister and Green were comfortable with the text, the last step was a review by the grant officer of Beloit College. After all this was completed, the final proposal was completed and submitted to the NEH in October 2005.[29]

All of this work, of course, resulted in the hard part of waiting for the NEH's reply, which culminated in a positive response in March 2006. This grant allocated $350,000 for the project and required an equal match. With the project starting in June, the Logan Museum staff had just two months to prepare. This included the hiring of staff to complete the project and movement forward in gathering the matching funds. These two steps and others were taken during this two-month window in building inertia for the two-year project. While the completion of this grant vastly improved the status of the collection, this one award did not end the museum's search for more support in fulfilling its mission. In fact, successful completion of the NEH grant actually paved the way for other grants. These included another NEH grant aimed at improving access to the Logan's collection of maps and also an Institute of Museum and Library Services (IMLS) Museums for America grant. The completion of the NEH grant by the Logan Museum, along with the other successes that followed, represents the steps taken and research required in obtaining and completing grants on large-scale federal levels.[30]

Photo 3.4. Improved storage of the ethnology collection after the grant.

Photo 3.5. Improved storage of the ethnology collection after the grant.

Greater Southwest Historical Museum

The Greater Southwest Historical Museum (GSHM), located in Ardmore, Oklahoma, collects and protects the material and cultural history of south-central Oklahoma. The museum's large Sam Noble Hall houses buildings and exhibits depicting daily life in Oklahoma at the turn of the century. Other wings of the gallery are dedicated to the evolution of transportation and include the Military Memorial Museum, aimed at presenting the story of local individuals who fought in this county's conflicts. Educational outreach opportunities include programs for children as well as workshops on teaching local history to educators. The collections of the organization include not only objects but also textiles and paper-based documentation of the past, such as personal letters, business records, and photographs.[31]

Originally GSHM operated entirely with an all-volunteer staff. However, in the early 2000s, the board of trustees began the process of hiring a full-time staff, which included a director, a curator of the collection, and maintenance employees. While this addition of full-time staff aided the GSHM, the uncataloged collection of approximately eighteen thousand objects remained a major issue. With no spare time and energy to take on such a massive undertaking, the organization considered a grant that would allow for this process to commence. In seeking funding, the organization utilized the experience of curator Kristin Mravinec, who had success with an IMLS grant at a previous organization.

Utilizing her past experience with IMLS and other research in the application process, Mravinec began drafting a proposal aimed at collections care. Incorporating additional text from director Michael Anderson, the application called for the hiring of staff devoted to cataloging ten thousand objects within a two-year period.[32] The grant would allow for newly hired staff as well as volunteers to catalog, assess condition, apply object identification numbers, and

Photo 3.6. Entrance into the Greater Southwest Historical Museum in Ardmore, Oklahoma.

enter the objects into the PastPerfect museum cataloging software.[33] Anderson stressed that, in the drafting of the proposal, any questions that arose should be referred to the IMLS staff. He noted it is much better to be informed about an incorrect approach to a grant in a quick phone conversation than in a formal rejection letter after months of hard labor.

The grant proposal was submitted to IMLS in 2007, and after six months of waiting, the GSHM learned of its successful grant application the late spring of 2008. The grant provided just over $75,000 to launch the cataloging project. The funds were issued four months later. This time allowed for the GSHM to issue the job notices for the program and for the process of reviewing applications to begin. In the fall of 2008, when the funds arrived, the GSHM commenced the cataloging project. The grant required matching funds; however, the majority of these dollars were covered by donated hours from volunteers and hours worked by the full-time staff.[34]

The grant is complete, and the GSHM is looking forward to future grants, including another IMLS grant to allow for the continuation of the cataloging process. The organized collection's benefits reach beyond simply gaining a hold on the large number of non-accessioned objects. The project has also greatly improved the community's view of the organization. Inquiries from past donors about the location or status of past donations of objects or collections of objects are now met with an informed reply. When asked for advice to small museums considering applying for a large grant, Anderson offered two thoughts: First, do not be intimidated by the process. Second, use the large array of available tools to help in your efforts, including networking with other small museum contacts, researching success stories of grant winners, and reading the large amount of literature on the subject of grant writing.[35]

Conclusion

Many possibilities exist for those interested in grants for small museums. Initiating this process may seem very overwhelming for those of us already strained by lack of staff hours and funding to cover just our basic duties. However, effective networking and researching can produce the needed information in beginning the relationship-building process that is so fundamental in acquiring grants. Having performed an institutional gut check, researched grant makers and grant winners, and worked smart in drafting the application materials, you will find that this effective use of time will produce successful grant awards. These awards can be stepping-stones that, when combined with other awards, programs, and exhibitions, place your organization on the path to your long-term goal of operating an outstanding small museum.

Resources

Books

Brophy, Sarah. *Is Your Museum Grant-Ready: Assessing Your Organization's Potential for Funding.* Oxford: AltaMira Press, 2005.

Collins, Jim. *Good to Great and the Social Sectors.* San Francisco: Elements Design Group, 2005.

Genoways, Hugh, and Lynne M. Ireland. *Museum Administration: An Introduction.* Oxford: AltaMira Press, 2003.

Wolf, Thomas. *Managing a Nonprofit Organization in the Twenty-First Century.* New York: Prentice Hall Press, 1999.

Newspapers

Bombardieri, Marcella, and Walter V. Robinson. "Wealthiest Nonprofits Favored by Foundations." *Boston Globe,* January 11, 2004. www.boston.com/news/nation/articles/2004/01/11/wealthiest_nonprofits_favored_by_foundations?pg=full (accessed August 14, 2011).

Websites and Web Pages

American Association for State and Local History (AASLH). "Statement of Professional Standards and Ethics." AASLH. www.aaslh.org/ethics.htm.

Greater Southwest Historical Museum (GSHM): www.gshm.org.

Institute of Museum and Library Services (IMLS). "News and Events." IMLS. www.imls.gov/news/2008/072208_list.shtm#OK.

Logan Museum. "Collections Accessibility Project." Logan Museum. www.beloit.edu/logan/collections/collections_project.php.

———. "Logan Museum of Anthropology." Logan Museum. www.beloit.edu/logan.

National Committee for Responsive Philanthropy (NCRP) and the Linchpin Campaign. "Seizing the Moment: Frank Advice for Community Organizers Who Want to Raise More Money." NCRP and the Linchpin Campaign. www.ncrp.org/files/publications/seizingthemoment.pdf.

Nonprofit Guides. "Grant-Writing Tools for Non-Profit Organizations." Nonprofit Guides. www.npquides.org/guide/index.html.

State of Rhode Island Historical Preservation and Heritage Commission (RIHPHC): www.preservation.ri.gov.

U.S. Department of Agriculture (USDA), "USDA National Agricultural Library Rural Information Center." USDA. www.nal.usda.gov/ric/ricpubs/fundguide.html.

U.S. Fulbright Online. "Preparing an Application in Writing." Fulbright. http://us.fulbrightonline.org/preparing_arts.html.

Author Interviews

Anderson, Michael, phone interview by author, Tempe, AZ, January 29, 2010.

Meister, Nicolette, phone interview by author, Tempe, AZ, January 27, 2010.

Notes

1. Jim Collins, *Good to Great and the Social Sectors* (San Francisco: Elements Design Group, 2005), 5.

2. Sarah Brophy, *Is Your Museum Grant-Ready? Assessing Your Organization's Potential for Funding* (Oxford: AltaMira Press, 2005), 53–71.

3. "USDA National Agricultural Library Rural Information Center," U.S. Department of Agriculture (USDA), www.nal.usda.gov/ric/ricpubs/fundguide.html.

4. Brophy, *Is Your Museum Grant-Ready?*, 11–19.

5. Marcella Bombardieri and Walter V. Robinson, "Wealthiest Nonprofits Favored by Foundations," *Boston Globe*, January 11, 2004, www.boston.com/news/nation/articles/2004/01/11/wealthiest_nonprofits_favored_by_foundations?pg=full (accessed August 14, 2011).

6. Bombardieri and Robinson, "Wealthiest Nonprofits."

7. Bombardieri and Robinson, "Wealthiest Nonprofits."

8. "Statement of Professional Standards and Ethics," American Association for State and Local History (AASLH), www.aaslh.org/ethics.htm.

9. AASLH, "Statement."

10. AASLH, "Statement."

11. Brophy, *Is Your Museum Grant-Ready?* 41–47.

12. Brophy, *Is Your Museum Grant-Ready?* 48–52.

13. AASLH, "Statement of Professional Standards and Ethics."

14. "Grant-Writing Tools for Non-Profit Organizations," Nonprofit Guides, www.npquides.org/guide/index.html.

15. Nonprofit Guides, "Grant-Writing Tools."

16. Nonprofit Guides, "Grant-Writing Tools."

17. Thomas Wolf, *Managing a Nonprofit Organization in the Twenty-First Century* (New York: Prentice Hall Press, 1999), 262–64.

18. Hugh H. Genoways and Lynne M. Ireland, *Museum Administration: An Introduction* (Oxford: AltaMira Press, 2003), 147.

19. "Preparing an Application in Writing," U.S. Fulbright Online, http://us.fulbrightonline.org/preparing_arts.html.

20. Collins, *Good to Great*, 23.

21. Collins, *Good to Great*, 23.

22. See the State of Rhode Island Historical Preservation & Heritage Commission website at www.preservation.ri.gov.

23. "Logan Museum of Anthropology," Logan Museum, www.beloit.edu/logan.

24. Nicolette Meister, phone interview by author, Tempe, AZ, January 27, 2010.

25. Meister, phone interview.

26. Meister, phone interview.

27. "Collections Accessibility Project," Logan Museum, www.beloit.edu/logan/collections/collections_project.php.

28. Logan Museum, "Collections Accessibility Project."

29. Logan Museum, "Collections Accessibility Project."

30. Logan Museum, "Collections Accessibility Project."

31. See the Greater Southwest Historical Museum website at www.gshm.org.

32. Michael Anderson, phone interview by author, Tempe, AZ, January 29, 2010.

33. "News and Events," Institute of Museum and Library Services, www.imls.gov/news/2008/072208_list.shtm#OK.

34. Anderson, phone interview.

35. Anderson, phone interview.

NOT ABOVE THE LAW:
MUSEUMS AND LEGAL ISSUES
Allyn Lord

Their chapter provides an overview of legal issues that museums may face. By no means does it include every area of law; nor can it treat each issue thoroughly. Instead, it provides a brief introduction to each issue and then guides you to resources for finding more information and legal rulings. The law is ever changing. For that reason, and because this book is intended to provide a jumping-off place for museums and not a reference for lawyers, court cases are not cited. Many of these will be found in the resources provided.

When it comes to legal issues for museums, ignorance is definitely not bliss. Instead, forewarned is forearmed. Make it a regular activity to research and seek advice before you deal with any legal issue. Along with learning how the law will impact your museum, policies and ethics are good prophylactics. Developing and implementing good policies that reflect applicable laws, regulations, and ethical standards can often prevent legal issues from arising or can mitigate their impact.

Disclaimer: The author is not an authority on the law, and this book is not a substitute for legal advice. Whenever you deal with legal issues, it is imperative that competent legal counsel be sought. In seeking out legal counsel, remember that many areas of museum law are specialty areas, from copyright and licensing to tax-exempt status and accessibility. An attorney who practices personal injury or bankruptcy law, for example, may not have the background or experience to deal with many museum concerns.

Founding and Governance Issues

Organizational Structures of Museums

A museum can be a private or public entity, and how it is legally classified determines under which set of laws it falls. Legally, a private museum may be classified as a trust, association, or corporation, while a public museum may be classified as either a charitable trust or corporation, or it may be a separate agency of a political or governmental "parent."[1] Most museums are considered charitable corporations, legal entities organized in a corporate form while having a charitable purpose, a kind of hybrid organization.

In a charitable corporation, the trustees (board members) hold legal title to property (real property as well as collections) for the benefit of others (either the general public or a broad segment of the public), and they can only use the property to pursue the corporation's charitable purposes. Trustees have great responsibility because they do not report to stockholders, as businesses do, but to the public.[2]

To deal with these responsibilities, as well as with the day-to-day legal concerns that may arise, retaining a qualified attorney is one way to shoulder the burden of governance. A lawyer can assist with a museum's incorporation and tax-exempt status, may provide advice on legal liabilities, and can explain trustees' legal responsibilities. A lawyer is also the point person for interpreting all laws and regulations, from local to federal, that impact your museum. Should your museum not have access to pro bono legal services, it will be well worth the money to hire such an attorney for advice and consultation, at least on an occasional basis.

Establishment and Maintenance of Federal Tax-Exempt Status

If your museum is a governmental agency or a political subdivision of a state, you are automatically exempt under the Internal Revenue Code (IRC) and need not file a tax return unless you receive unrelated business taxable income[3] (see "Unrelated Business Income Tax" below). If your museum decides not to incorporate, it will be treated by the Internal Revenue Service (IRS) as a charitable trust.[4] Otherwise, you most likely will seek tax-exempt status under Section 501(c)(3) of the IRC. Such status not only means you are exempt from paying federal taxes but also allows your donors to receive tax benefits from their gifts to the museum.

First, articles of incorporation that describe your museum, its operations, and its authority must be prepared with an attorney and filed with your state's secretary of state. You will also need bylaws, your internal regulations, which trustees and the director draw up, often in consultation with an attorney. Once you receive your certificate of incorporation, you may apply to the IRS for tax-exempt status by filing Form 1023. For more information on the process, check with the revenue department of your state or see *Museums and the Law*.[5] Tax exemption must also be sought at the state and local levels, which may release your museum from real property taxes, state income tax, and state and local sales tax on purchased items.[6]

Once recognition of tax-exempt status is received, you will normally remain exempt as long as your mission and activities do not conflict with the IRC's exemption status.[7] Because the IRC allows the tax exemption and donor tax benefit only if your museum is "organized and operated exclusively for one or more of the purposes enumerated as allowed by the federal regulations governing tax-exempt organizations,"[8] your articles of incorporation or other enabling legislation should specifically refer to those purposes. For tests to determine whether a museum is operating exclusively for charitable purposes, see *Museums and the Law*.[9] For a tutorial on tax basics for tax-exempt organizations, see the IRS publication "Stay Exempt: Tax Basics for Exempt Organizations."[10]

IRC Section 501 exempt organizations whose annual receipts are "normally" more than $50,000 must file an annual information return, itemizing receipts and expenditures and indicating current financial status. This is usually done by submitting Form 990, "Return of Organization Exempt from Income Tax."[11] (See the section on record keeping and compliance in chapter 1 of this book.) Many states also require supplemental reports as well as Form 990. Form 990 is a public document that is open to public viewing and is now being posted on the Internet by the National Center for Charitable Statistics and Guidestar. For more information about public disclosure regarding tax-exempt organizations, see the IRS Web page "FAQs about the Exempt Organization Public Disclosure Requirements."[12] For more on Form 990 and related material, see "How to Read the IRS Form 990 & Find Out What It Means."[13] The Urban Institute website provides online and free technical support for nonprofits working on 990s.[14]

Governance Responsibilities

Standards of Conduct

With increased scrutiny of corporations by stockholders, the public, and the federal government, charitable corporations are also seeing increased interest in their standards of conduct. Museum trustees, therefore, must be increasingly aware of their legal and fiduciary responsibilities. "Under the traditional trustee test, good faith will not save a trustee who fails to perform as 'a man of ordinary prudence' in carrying out the required duties."[15] Museum boards of trustees are charged with three core duties: care, loyalty, and obedience. Duty of care means "good-faith efforts on the part of board members to set reasonable policy, to follow policy, and to exercise reasonable oversight,"[16] avoiding gross negligence and purposeful wrongdoing. Duty of loyalty entails a clear and determined avoidance of conflict of interest (see "Conflicts of Interest" below). Duty of obedience means making every decision with particular focus on the museum mission and the board's fiduciary responsibilities.[17]

Conflicts of Interest

While conflicts of interest are, in essence, ethical matters, when problems arise in that area, the resolution may turn into a legal issue. Conflict-of-interest issues include such subjects as receipt of gifts and favors, outside employment, personal collecting, purchases of museum property or collections, and confidentiality. These issues should be addressed in a museum's code of ethics[18] and should be dealt with transparently and through full disclosure (e.g., a signed policy by each board member or recusal from board matters where a conflict of interest exists).

Legal Responsibilities

Board members are "the stewards or guardians of the public interest claimed by the organization at its founding and for which the state is willing to confer certain benefits, including tax exemption."[19] Although there is no expectation that board members will be experts in any field of law, neither can trustees delegate their legal responsibilities to others. A board's legal responsibilities include, but are not limited to, complying with federal, state, and local laws and regulations; timely reporting to appropriate governmental agencies; recording of any lobbying activities; complying with safety, health, labor, and other standards; providing personnel policies and procedures; adhering to articles of incorporation and bylaws; undertaking an annual audit; and providing applicable information under the Freedom of Information Act (FOIA).[20]

Financial Responsibilities

Museum trustees' duty of care to their museum includes a fiduciary responsibility for finances that, like their legal responsibility, cannot be delegated to others and is owed to the public for the public benefit. Therefore, trustees are publicly accountable and must pay close attention to museum finances, endowment activities, and financial procedures, policies, and reports. Financial malfeasance (misconduct) and nonfeasance (failure to perform an official duty) can be charged against a board for a myriad of activities. These can include, for example, "failing to monitor key indicators, allowing the [museum] to drift into financial trouble; failing to pay sufficient attention to whether the [museum's] financial resources are being effectively spent on programs; [and] being too trusting of staff who handle money."[21] Your state's attorney general has oversight and enforcement in regard to charitable corporations.[22]

Numerous actions may help to minimize your museum's financial liability. Some of these include obtaining an annual audited financial statement; issuing periodic interim financial reports to the board; approving an annual budget;

implementing internal financial and bookkeeping procedures approved by the board and periodically reviewed; putting procedures in place to assure control of cash; and having short- and long-term plans for investment, reviewed periodically by the board.[23] See chapter 1 in this book for more information on good financial management.

Protections against Liability

Many museums include in their bylaws indemnification language that indicates the museum's intent to cover the expenses of a board member in defending an action or paying a settlement related to that member's board service.[24] A directors and officers (D&O) insurance policy safeguards board members and your museum for actions not covered by a general liability policy. For a more thorough discussion of D&O insurance, see "Nuts and Bolts of Insurance: Directors and Officers Liability and Media Liability."[25]

Although museums typically do not undergo frequent IRS audits, it may be prudent to conduct regular self-audits to keep the risks of an audit at bay. This can be done by regularly reviewing (preferably annually at a board retreat or finance committee annual meeting) activities in high-profile or high-risk areas.[26]

Many boards consider young people for board membership. A few states prohibit minors from serving on boards, so it would be prudent to check your state's regulations for board membership age limits. Additionally, many states do not allow minors to sign binding contracts. If young people do serve on your board, do not allow them to sign such contracts and avoid their election to positions dealing with financial matters. Some D&O insurance policies may exclude minors. An alternative to board membership for minors is service on an advisory committee or council.[27]

Common thinking to the contrary, museums can engage in legislative advocacy for themselves. Such advocacy is not prohibited by law, and in fact many legislators are more than happy to meet with museum advocates. For information about and rules for advocacy, see "Nonprofits and Government: What You Can and Can't Do."[28]

Freedom of Information

The Freedom of Information Act was enacted to give the public greater access to federal governmental records, and the Electronic Freedom of Information Act Amendments expanded FOIA's scope to include electronic records.[29] The Freedom of Information Act reference guide can be found at the U.S. Department of Justice's FOIA website.[30] The FOIA does not apply to records of state or local governments, but all state governments have their own FOIA-type statutes. These may be obtained by contacting your state's attorney general.[31]

Meetings

Museum boards of trustees are required to meet, annually at minimum. Sources of liability regarding these meetings include, but are not limited to, a notice and agenda distributed in advance to attendees, discussions of subjects with potentially adverse legal ramifications, the taking of and responsibility for minutes, and "off-the-record" meetings. For more information, see the American Association of Museums' (AAM) "Insurability Checklist."[32]

Support Organizations

Museum friends groups provide various kinds of support for museums, such as volunteer labor, grant sponsorship, special events, and other kinds of fundraising. Such groups are usually incorporated as separate 501(c)(3) organizations and have their own missions, bylaws, finances, and boards. For a discussion of friends groups, including teen friends, see "Friends & Foundations Fact Sheets."[33] The World Federation of Friends of Museums has additional information about friends groups, including such resources as a code of ethics.[34]

If your 501(c)(3) museum wants to conduct activities that do not fall within the scope of your present charter, you might move those activities to a separate organization. Sometimes that new organization may not qualify for its own tax-exempt status. An option is to create a charitable support organization under IRC 509(a)(3). Such an organization is not tax exempt itself but piggybacks on your 501(c)(3) exempt status. For more on a 509(a)(3) organization, see "Charitable Support Tax Exempt Organizations."[35]

Financial, Contractual, and Tax Issues

Tax Issues

Tax laws are constantly changing, making it difficult for nonprofit organizations to keep track of issues such as tax deductions, valuations of gifts, annuities, and charitable deductions. For a thorough and up-to-date treatment of all areas of tax information, including links to IRS codes, regulations, private letter rulings, and court cases, see GiftLaw Pro.[36]

Unrelated Business Income Tax

The IRS mandates that income produced at exempt organizations from "regularly conducted activities," such as those conducted by museum stores and restaurants (as opposed to one-time or occasional activities such as fundraising events), be related to the organization's exempt purpose or else become subject to the unrelated business income tax (UBIT). UBIT was established to protect nonexempt businesses from unfair competition. If a "substantial" percentage of a museum's income comes from unrelated activities, it risks losing its tax-exempt status. And even if, for example, some museum store merchandise is substantially related to the museum's mission, the IRS's so-called fragmentation rule means that other merchandise that is not so related can be separated out for taxation.[37] Although the IRS has not ruled on the definition of "substantial," "as a general rule . . . if unrelated income regularly falls within the range of 15–30% of museum revenues, you may wish to establish a for-profit subsidiary."[38]

While more details about UBIT regulations are available on the IRS website,[39] a few rulings on UBIT regarding museum stores may be informative. Low-cost items (e.g., T-shirts, magnets) are not taxable if they promote the museum or provide an educational message.[40] The sale of note cards or postcards featuring images of museum collections has been deemed to be within the law.[41] "Merely affixing the museum's name to an object [however] did not establish the requisite causal relationship with the museum's exempt purpose. It makes no difference that many of the articles containing the name or logo are inexpensive souvenirs or trinkets."[42]

There are some general rules about buying and producing merchandise to sell in a museum store with respect to UBIT. First, each sale item will be individually considered for UBIT by the IRS. Thus, "it can be helpful to consult curators and educators to evaluate which goods are related to the museum's purposes and which are not."[43] Merchandise featuring the reproduction of something in the museum collections is less likely to fall under UBIT. Second, adding an accompanying small card or hang tag with educational information about the item (e.g., information about the artist, historical information about the craft, how the item relates to local history) increases the educational value and thus helps negate UBIT. Third, you can sell unrelated merchandise, but you will have to keep track of these sales in order to pay UBIT.[44]

There are a few other notes regarding legal issues and museum stores. Under the Federal Trade Commission Act, store advertising "must be truthful and non-deceptive; advertisers must have evidence to back up their claims; and advertisements cannot be unfair."[45] If your store is online, you also need to think about fraud prevention (see "Preventing Fraud on Your Web Site"[46]) and keep updated on taxes for Internet sales.[47]

There are three major exclusions to UBIT regulations on food and beverages at museums. First, restaurants, cafés, and vending machines are exempt according to the "convenience exception" for on-site sales of items that enable visitors to spend more time at the museum.[48] However, "a dining facility [that] is accessible not only through the museum but also through a door directly to the street . . . has been held by the IRS not to be primarily for visitor convenience but for general public use, and therefore taxable."[49] Second, use of museum facilities for "social affairs" has been deemed permissible if the event is held primarily for museum or educational purposes.[50] Third, property rental for functions by outside organizations is considered "passive revenue" and, as such, is excluded from UBIT. "However, if a museum provides services, such as labor, food, catering, linens, etc., in addition to simply renting out a facility then the rental arrangement is subject to tax."[51]

In addition to UBIT concerns on food service, there are also issues of food safety, retail food production, and food codes under the jurisdiction of the Food and Drug Administration (FDA). Federal codes and ordinances can be found at the FDA's food-code Web page,[52] while information on retail (e.g., restaurant, café, food cart, etc.) food protection can be found at the FDA's retail food-protection Web page.[53]

Parking lots that charge fees are considered necessary for a museum to attract visitors and thereby fall outside UBIT. However, a museum "must be careful of the danger of permitting a 'dual use' of its parking facility by encouraging (or allowing) individuals unrelated to the museum to park for a fee."[54]

Museum-sponsored travel tours must also be in keeping with a museum's exempt purposes in order to avoid UBIT. Such activities as how the destination was chosen and the actual conduct of the tour must be clearly shown to be "substantially related."[55]

Accounting and Audits

An audit determines whether a museum's financial statements are complete and accurate. Some nonprofits are legally required to obtain an audit if, for instance, they receive contributions over a specified amount or hire a paid fundraiser; check with your state's attorney general or secretary of state to determine your state's regulations. In compliance with the Single Audit Act and OMB Circular A-133: Audits of States, Local Governments, and Nonprofit Organizations, if your museum receives $500,000 or more in federal money (directly or from pass-through grants) in a single year, you are required to conduct an audit.[56] In response to the 2002 Sarbanes-Oxley Act, many museums have established an audit committee or, often for smaller museums, a finance/audit committee.[57] Short of these requirements, there exist less rigorous or costly alternatives to an audit that provide some degree of accountability.[58] "A frequently cited guide for moving to annual audits, rather than financial reviews, is when a nonprofit's budget reaches around $350,000."[59]

The Governmental Accounting Standards Board (GASB) establishes standards for financial accounting and reporting for state and local governments. GASB publications, on such topics as auditing standards, fund balance reporting, and basic financial statements, can be ordered through the GASB store,[60] and "plain-language summaries" of GASB standards and projects can be downloaded for free.[61]

The Financial Accounting Standards Board (FASB) is the designated non-governmental organization for setting financial accounting standards through FASB Accounting Standards Codification.[62] The standards are browsable by topic free of charge.[63]

Auditing standards require auditors to review the tax-exempt status of your museum and identify any activities that may endanger it. Auditors should also verify that taxes and reports are filed properly and on time. For help with audits, see the Virginia Society of Certified Public Accountants website and its free audit guide for small nonprofit organizations.[64] For steps museums can take to minimize the cost of these audits, see "New Auditing Standards and How They May Impact Your Organization."[65]

FASB requires nonprofit organizations to report assets and statements of activity for three funds: unrestricted funds, which can be used for any purpose (e.g., current operating funds, board-designated (project) funds, and board-designated quasi-endowment funds); temporarily restricted funds; and permanently restricted funds. Both types of restricted funds can only be used for designated purposes (e.g., donor-restricted funds, grants, and true endowment funds). For more on accounting requirements and endowments, see "Creating and Building Endowments for Small Museums."[66]

Receipt of Federal Financial Assistance

Federal financial assistance—whether received directly from a government grant, loan, or other source or indirectly via a state or municipal pass-through entity—can make a big difference to a museum, especially a small museum. However, receipt of such funds is usually accompanied by other layers of oversight and activity, requiring compliance with certain regulations or engagement in certain activities and making the museum liable if such requirements are not met. The federal laws and regulations with which you must comply involve the areas of civil rights, drug avoidance, and lobbying activity. For more information on these areas, see *A Legal Primer on Managing Museum Collections*.[67]

Contracts and Licensing Agreements

A contract is an agreement that creates obligations. In developing contracts, one goal is to place the liability risk on the other party through "contractual representations, indemnifications, releases, and waivers."[68]

Contract law is a voluminous subject. For information on contracts, enforceability, contract conditions, voiding a contract, and contract authority, see "A Contract Law Primer for the Museum Administrator."[69] For information on contracts and memoranda of agreement and how to read, write, and understand them, see "Understanding and Writing Contracts and Memoranda of Agreement."[70]

One specific kind of contract a museum may use is a catering contract, which should include information on the museum's policies, insurance requirements, and provisions for termination should policies not be followed. You should always check references for caterers to verify that they are licensed by the local health department.[71]

Another specialized kind of contract for museums is a licensing agreement, which is called for whenever someone wants to use or reproduce "content." Content could include, but is not limited to, artworks and objects in your collections, brochures, logos, websites, photographs, reports, documents, books, and audio recordings, including both traditional and digital media. Licensing the use of this content can provide revenue and expand your museum's reach, but there are many issues to decide when considering an agreement.

Most importantly, you must determine what rights you have for the item in question. Simply because you have the item in your collections does not mean you have the right to license it. If the creator or author of the item is still alive, you must secure his or her permission, unless it has been legally transferred to you in writing; if this person is not living, you will need to track down heirs or assignees for permission (see the discussion of rights on page 109). For more on determining licensing rights, see "Museum Licensing: How to Do It Right!"[72]

As for the agreement itself, there is currently no standard document. A licensing agreement may set boundaries on the product's sale or may limit the manufacturer to a specific design. "The agreement should contain clauses regarding assignability, termination, option to renew, and right of the museum to reject any product both initially and throughout the terms of the agreement. The museum should be the sole judge of whether a product has met the standards of quality established by the parties."[73] For more on licensing agreements and how to set them up, see "A Canadian Museum's Guide to Developing a Licensing Strategy."[74] For your own licensing, which may be beyond the expertise or time of your museum, you may want to sign a licensing agreement with a reputable firm.

Music is omnipresent in most museums, from exhibits to programs, from restaurants to museum stores. Many fail to realize that U.S. copyright law makes it illegal to play or perform music in public places without the permission of the copyright owner and the payment of a licensing fee. Subscription-based online music stores provide on-demand music licensing and many offer generous policies for noncommercial projects. The best resource to guide you in determining how legal it is to play music is the AAM's "Music Licensing for Museums."[75] For any licensing that must occur, there are three performance rights licensing organizations: the American Society of Composers, Authors, and Publishers (www.ascap.com); Broadcast Music, Inc. (www.bmi.com); and SESAC (www.sesac.com).

Credit Cards

If your museum accepts payment by credit card, especially via the Internet, for museum store purchases, memberships, and the like, you must consider your credit card equipment and the safety of your customers' sensitive information. Given the recent rise of credit card and identity theft, as well as other criminal online activities, recent rules and laws have been passed governing how personal information is to be protected and when organizations are obligated to report a breach. The Payment Card Industry (PCI) Data Security Standard and state identity theft and breach notification laws offer guidelines for securing credit card information.[76] Failure to comply with the PCI standard that results in a security breach may result in a fine by the bank that processes your museum's transactions.[77] Contact your bank or card processor to determine your compliance responsibilities.

For museums without the security or information technology expertise on staff to meet PCI compliance, there are a couple of alternatives. Perhaps the easiest system is to use a third-party service to handle the credit card processing for you; the service will deal with the personal credit card information and thus must be PCI compliant, not you. Ask your bank for a referral to a reputable company. Another option is to use PayPal instead of credit cards. PayPal brokers payments from one account holder to another over the Internet and sends the money to the museum's account for a percentage of the transaction and a small fee. For information on these options and for rules to comply with PCI, see "Laws for Organizations That Accept Online Payments."[78]

Fundraising

Many states and some municipal or other local governments require organizations soliciting charitable contributions to register before solicitations occur and to file periodic financial reports, although there are some exemptions.[79] To determine if your state requires registration, check with the National Association of State Charity Officials.[80] Laws for fundraising via the Internet, including "passive fundraising" (the mere presence of a request for funds on your museum website), have yet to be settled; check with your legal counsel and with your state's charity official to determine whether you need to register for Internet fundraising.[81]

If your fundraising involves raffles or sweepstakes-type promotions, it would be wise to check with your state's attorney general[82] to determine whether state laws concerning disclosure and licensing apply.

Whatever method of solicitation you use, tax law states that donors cannot receive goods or services in return for their gifts or dividends on their investment. Small tokens of appreciation and recognition pass muster, but a monetary return for gifts can cause loss of tax deduction for the donor and trigger a loss of tax exemption for the museum.[83]

Corporate sponsorships can provide major financial support for, and increase the visibility of, your museum. However, there are legal and ethical issues, as well as tax consequences, to consider when seeking such sponsorships.[84] Tax laws mandate that income from activities that are not "substantially" related to the museum's mission are subject to UBIT (see "Unrelated Business Income Tax" on pages 86–88). However, if a business makes "qualified sponsorship payments" to your museum "for which there is no expectation of a substantial return benefit," those payments are not subject to UBIT. To learn more about "qualified sponsorship payments," see "'Tis the Season for Corporate Sponsorship."[85] Even the method you choose to acknowledge a corporate sponsorship may trigger UBIT, and the distinction between that acknowledgment and advertising is a key issue, especially regarding what could be considered a "substantial return benefit" to the corporation.[86] Additionally, only "insubstantial" benefits may accrue to the corporate sponsor in return for the sponsorship, so special gifts, private viewings, and other high-priced or highly sought benefits would also trigger UBIT.[87] Even for relatively small amounts of corporate support, a contract is in order to outline and detail the responsibilities of both the museum and sponsor.[88]

If your museum is seeking corporate sponsorships as a regular part of its fundraising, it would be worthwhile for your board to have a discussion and develop guidelines to deal with such relationships. "Ultimately, the museum's board of trustees has the responsibility to accept or reject corporate sponsorship offers. In doing so, the trustees should always consider whether a given corporate sponsorship agreement complies with the museum's ethical standards as well as any applicable local, state and federal laws."[89]

Real Estate

Property tax exemptions vary by municipality, county, and state and are often available, both for real estate and personal property, for charitable organizations. Some exemptions require annual filings.[90]

Gifts of real estate to your museum may be generous, but there are several liability issues to consider. Donated property with environmental problems (e.g., hazardous materials, soil or water pollutants) fall under the Comprehensive Environmental Response, Compensation and Liability Act (CERCLA),[91] which will charge your museum with cleanup costs that may far exceed the value of the gift. Gifts of real estate can also divert the focus of your museum if the property is not consistent with your mission. For more on real estate gifts and what to look and look out for, see "Understanding and Drafting Nonprofit Gift Acceptance Policies."[92]

Human Resources and the Law

The volume of laws, statutes, and regulations surrounding human resource issues is staggering. Only the most basic of museum-related issues can be itemized here. An excellent overall resource is the Department of Labor's "Employment Law Guide: Laws, Regulations, and Technical Assistance Services," which describes the major statutes and regulations administered by the U.S. Department of Labor that affect businesses and workers.[93] Topics include minimum wage and overtime pay, the Occupational Safety and Health Act (OSHA), employee benefits, whistle-blower and retaliation protections, and federal contracts. Three helpful guides to human resource information are the "Employment Law Guide for Non-Profit Organizations,"[94] the "FirstStep Employment Law Advisor,"[95] and the "Checklist of Human Resource Management Indicators for Nonprofit Organizations."[96]

Discrimination in Employment

According to federal law, a museum may not consider a job applicant's race, color, religion, sex (including pregnancy), national origin, age (forty or older), disability, or genetic information when hiring. However, depending upon the number of employees, an employer may not be covered by these federal laws; see the website of the Equal Employment Opportunity Commission (EEOC) first to determine if your museum is covered.[97] In addition, most states and some localities prohibit employment discrimination in hiring on the basis of other protected characteristics, such as name or marital status, sexual orientation, or military service.[98] All interview questions must avoid direct inquiries or inferences about these categories; using a list of inquiry guidelines can make the interview process easier.[99] The EEOC enforces the laws and provides oversight and assistance, including "Employers" pages on its website with much helpful information, some targeted at small businesses and organizations without a human resources department.[100]

Title VI of the Civil Rights Act prohibits discrimination on the basis of race, color, or national origin in programs and activities that receive federal financial assistance. Title VII of the act prohibits discrimination in hiring, promotion, discharge, pay, fringe benefits, job training, classification, referral, and other aspects of employment, on the basis of race, color, religion, sex, or national origin. Title IX of the Education Amendments of 1972 prohibits discrimination on the basis of sex in educational programs and activities that receive federal financial assistance.[101]

The Age Discrimination in Employment Act (ADEA) protects certain applicants and employees forty years of age and older from discrimination on the basis of age in hiring, promotion, discharge, compensation, and terms, conditions, or privileges of employment.[102] A later Age Discrimination Act prohibits discrimination on the basis of age in programs and activities receiving federal financial assistance. Interview questions that ask about age directly or indirectly (e.g., asking what year an applicant graduated from high school or college) are prohibited.[103]

Among other regulations, the Fair Labor Standards Act (FLSA) sets the minimum age for employment (fourteen for nonagricultural jobs) and restricts the hours that those under age sixteen may work.[104]

Employers with fifteen or more employees are prohibited from discriminating against people with disabilities by Title I of the Americans with Disabilities Act (ADA).[105] The ADA requires nondiscrimination in hiring qualified applicants with disabilities, job accommodation for applicants and workers with disabilities when such accommodations do not impose "undue hardship," and equal opportunity in promotion and benefits.[106]

The Genetic Information Nondiscrimination Act prohibits discrimination based on genetic information (e.g., a family history of cancer or sickle cell anemia).[107] Employers may not disclose genetic information about applicants or employees and must keep genetic information confidential and in a separate medical file; there are limited exceptions to this nondisclosure rule.[108]

An applicant's marital status is considered gender-specific information; therefore, since federal and state laws prohibit discrimination in hiring based on sex, employers are prohibited from asking about an applicant's maiden name or marital status.[109]

The Uniformed Services Employment and Reemployment Rights Act[110] protects service members' reemployment rights when returning from a period of service in the uniformed services and prohibits employer discrimination based on military service or obligation.

Accompanying Title VII of the Civil Rights Act, which prohibits discrimination in employment based on national origin, the Immigration and Nationality Act prohibits employers from discriminating based on national origin against U.S. citizens, U.S. nationals, and authorized aliens; it also prohibits discrimination based on citizenship status against U.S. citizens, U.S. nationals, and some classes of aliens with work authorization.[111] Additionally, the Immigration Reform and Control Act (IRCA), applicable to employers with four or more employees, prohibits intentional discrimination on the basis of national origin or citizenship status. IRCA also requires employers to verify the work eligibility status of all new hires.[112]

Federal contractors and subcontractors are required by EEOC and affirmative action guidelines to "recruit and advance qualified minorities, women, persons with disabilities, and covered veterans."[113]

Sexual Harassment

Sexual harassment is a form of sex discrimination that falls under the protection of Title VII of the Civil Rights Act, which applies to employers with fifteen or more employees; employees of smaller businesses and organizations are typically protected by similar state antidiscrimination laws.[114] Federal law also protects same-sex sexual harassment, while state laws vary on the issue. The EEOC defines sexual harassment as "unwelcome sexual advances, requests for sexual favors, and other verbal or physical conduct of a sexual nature . . . when submission to or rejection of this conduct explicitly or implicitly affects an individual's employment, unreasonably interferes with an individual's work performance, or creates an intimidating, hostile or offensive work environment."[115]

Sexual harassment relates to many aspects of employment, including hiring, promotions, dismissals, raises, benefits, leaves of absence, and work assignments. The offense is gender neutral; both a woman and a man can be a victim or a harasser. The victim does not actually have to be the one harassed but could be someone affected by the conduct. The harasser can be the victim's supervisor, a supervisor in another area, a coworker, someone contracted by the employer, or a nonemployee. In all cases, the harasser's conduct is unwelcome.[116]

Sexual harassment may occur when an employee is required to tolerate it in order to keep a job, benefit, raise, or promotion (so-called quid pro quo harassment) or when it "unreasonably interferes with or alters the employee's work performance, or creates a hostile, abusive, or offensive work environment."[117] For more information, see the EEOC's "Policy Guidance on Current Issues of Sexual Harassment."[118]

Whistle-Blower Protection

Your museum should have policies and procedures in place that encourage employees to come forward as soon as possible with credible information on workplace violations or illegal practices. But employees and volunteers need to feel safe in reporting this kind of behavior, or "whistle-blowing." Whistle-blowers are protected from retaliation by their employers by a number of laws, including OSHA, which covers complaints about "unsafe or unhealthful conditions in the workplace, environmental problems, [and] certain public safety hazards. . . . Whistle-blowers may not be transferred, denied a raise, have their hours reduced, or be fired or punished in any other way because they have exercised any right afforded to them under one of the laws that protect whistle-blowers."[119]

Employment at Will

Under at-will employment, an employer may fire any employee for any reason or no reason, as long as the termination is not unlawful or discriminatory (based on age, sex, national origin, or disability). For more on at-will employment and agreements, see "Employment at Will: What Does It Mean?"[120] To determine if your museum is located in an at-will employment state, see "Employment At Will States."[121]

Wages

The Fair Labor Standards Act establishes minimum wage, overtime pay, record keeping, and youth-employment standards affecting employees in the private sector and in federal, state, and local governments. Overtime pay at a rate not less than one and a half times the regular rate of pay is required after forty hours of work in a workweek.[122] To keep track of the current minimum wage, see the U.S. Department of Labor's minimum wage site.[123]

Work Hours

Federal law does not require lunch or coffee breaks. When given, however, short breaks (typically five to twenty minutes) are considered compensable (paid) work hours. Meal periods (of at least thirty minutes) are not considered work time and are not compensable.[124]

While time spent traveling to and from work is generally not considered work time, travel time during normal work hours is counted as compensable.[125]

Benefits

Many employee benefits, such as life insurance, medical insurance accounts, and wellness benefits, are not a matter of law but generally a matter of agreement between an employer and an employee.

Health Plans

Most private-sector health plans are covered by the Employee Retirement Income Security Act (ERISA), which sets uniform minimum standards to ensure that employee benefit plans are established and maintained in a fair and financially sound manner.[126] For compliance assistance materials and record-keeping information, see the U.S. Department of Labor's "Health Benefits."

Workers' Compensation

Workers' compensation laws were enacted to financially assist employees who are injured or disabled on the job and to provide benefits for dependents of those employees killed due to work-related illness or accidents. Federal, nonmilitary workers and other classes of workers (nonmuseum) are covered by federal workers' compensation programs,[127] while most employees' workers' compensation benefits fall under state laws and statutes. To learn what your state offers in workers' compensation, see "State Workers' Compensation Offices."[128]

Leave Benefits

Employees use leave to take time off from work. The extent of the leave and whether it is paid are generally matters of agreement between an employer and an employee. Many types of leave fall under this employer-regulated category, such as vacations, holidays, funeral leave, jury duty, and sick leave.[129]

The Family and Medical Leave Act (FMLA)[130] provides up to twelve weeks of unpaid, job-protected leave per year for certain employees. The act also requires that the employee continue her or his group health benefits during the leave. Among others, the FMLA applies to all public agencies and companies with fifty or more employees. For more information on FMLA, compliance, and additional rulings, see the Department of Labor's "Family & Medical Leave."

Termination

Workers' rights following termination include the right to continue group health benefits for a limited period under the Consolidated Omnibus Budget Reconciliation Act (COBRA)[131] and the Health Insurance Portability and Accountability Act (HIPAA).[132] Employers may be required to provide notices about this right to their employees. Employees "who are unemployed through no fault of their own (as determined under state law), and meet other eligibility requirements, may be eligible to receive unemployment benefits."[133] For more on court cases surrounding termination of employment, see *Museums and the Law*.[134]

Personnel Files

Every employer covered by the Fair Labor Standards Act[135] must retain a number of records for each covered, nonexempt worker. Accurate information about the employee and data about hours worked and wages earned must be included. For a list of records to be maintained by the employer, see "Recordkeeping & Reporting on the Department of Labor's website."[136]

Retirement Plans

There are many different types of retirement plans, including the 401(k) and the traditional pension (aka a defined benefit plan). These employee-benefit plans are maintained by employers, and they provide retirement income or defer income until termination of employment or beyond. Most private-sector pension plans are under ERISA,[137] which provides protections for participants and their beneficiaries in employee benefit plans.

Independent Contractors

Contracts for assistance from outside the museum are legally enforceable documents that help a museum maintain control over the quality of supplies and services it receives.[138] Contractors can include accountants, appraisers, architects, conservators, executive search consultants, exhibit contractors, fundraising consultants, graphic designers, guest curators, legal counsel, management consultants, planning consultants, program evaluators, security consultants, and technology consultants.[139]

The differences between an independent contractor and an employee are important. "Generally, you must withhold income taxes, withhold and pay Social Security and Medicare taxes, and pay unemployment tax on wages paid to an employee. You do not generally have to withhold or pay any taxes on payments to independent contractors."[140] To help make this determination and for information on employment tax obligations, see the IRS publication "Independent Contractor (Self-Employed) or Employee?"[141] or the Department of Labor's "Employment Relationship under the Fair Labor Standards Act (FLSA)."[142] Many organizations such as museums prefer to contract out functions that are not directly related to their core mission (e.g., custodial or food service).

Volunteers

Volunteers are the lifeblood of almost every museum, especially small museums, where some are solely volunteer run. While there are laws on every level that deal with volunteers and volunteer liability, the major way your museum can protect its volunteers and you is by first screening potential volunteers as you do employee applicants. Volunteers who undertake high-risk jobs need particular attention, whether they are working with children, assisting with collections, or perhaps driving for trips or deliveries. Having written position descriptions for every volunteer assignment also makes very clear exactly what the volunteer assignment is, what the expectations are, and the volunteer's prohibitions and the consequences. Lastly, adequate supervision of volunteers undertaking riskier jobs may also help decrease accidents and incidents.

The federal Volunteer Protection Act (VPA)[143] "provides that, if a volunteer meets certain criteria, he or she shall not be liable for simple negligence while acting on behalf of a nonprofit or governmental organization. The VPA also provides some limitations on the assessment of non-economic losses and punitive damages against a volunteer."[144] However, the VPA does not protect a volunteer from liability for harm "caused by willful or criminal misconduct, gross negligence, reckless misconduct, or a conscious, flagrant indifference to the rights or safety of the individual harmed by the volunteer action."[145] The act does allow for lawsuits against volunteers and against your museum.

Every state has a volunteer protection law, but they differ widely and have numerous exceptions.[146]

Depending on individual state laws governing volunteer liability, your museum may want to consider providing insurance or indemnification for volunteers as you may do for board members. Insurance may be a factor, for example, for accident injuries on-site or in the community, vehicle accidents in the course of performing volunteer work, or bonding for those who handle money (e.g., museum store volunteers).[147] There are also many liability issues surrounding volunteers who have access to the Internet and e-mail through your museum.[148]

If your museum has a separate volunteer organization, you may have additional legal liabilities. "To minimize the legal liability of the museum and the volunteer group, a museum must exercise some means of control over its volunteer organization. Four areas merit attention: using the museum's name; raising money; using the museum's paid staff to assist the volunteer organization's programs; and undertaking certain types of activities."[149] As in other areas, advice from legal counsel in creating an agreement between the museum and the volunteer organization can help minimize or mitigate legal liability.

Intellectual Property: Employees' Work

On a regular basis, museum employees create new programs, research new information, author museum-related articles, develop new products, and build new kinds of exhibits. These work products, called "intellectual property," that are created, researched, authored, developed, and built in the course of an employee's work at the museum belong, by U.S. copyright law, to the museum, not to the employee (see "Copyright" below). The duration of the copyright, however, "is measured with reference to the life of the employed creator."[150]

As an example, note that the Royal Ontario Museum (ROM) includes in its "Board Policy: Copyright," this statement: "The ROM owns the economic rights in works produced by employees as part of their employment duties, in the absence of an agreement to the contrary. Also, as the ROM owns its collections and other resources, the ROM will have interests to economic rights in works derived, in whole or in part, from the use of these resources."[151]

Records Retention

While your museum (or your museum's "parent") may have a records retention policy, a number of federal laws mandate explicit or implicit record-keeping requirements that you should be sure are covered in your policy. Among the rules already discussed are the ADA, FMLA, FLSA, Title VII of the Civil Rights Act, OSHA, and ERISA. Other laws with record-keeping requirements include the ADEA, Equal Pay Act, and IRCA. For a list that addresses types of records, length of time those records must be retained, and the law requiring records retention, see "Human Resources Software: Legal Issues."[152] For state laws related to record keeping for wage and hour requirements and payroll taxes, see Business Owner's Toolkit, "Recordkeeping Requirements."[153] For a sample document retention and destruction policy, see the Volunteer Lawyers & Accountants for the Arts' "Sample Document Retention and Destruction Policy."[154] For tips on developing a strategy to manage electronic records, see the Minnesota Historical Society's "Electronic Records Management Guidelines."[155] For dealing with e-mail records, see the Smithsonian Institution Archives, "Treating Email As Records."[156]

The Sarbanes-Oxley Act of 2002 addresses accounting and investment firms and large public corporations, but it is likely that the rules adopted therein may be extended to private businesses and nonprofit organizations.[157]

Collections and the Law

Acquisition and Ownership

Clear Title

No matter how your museum acquires collections, your goal should be to have clear title and, in most cases, complete title to those collections. To have clear and complete title, that is, to be in possession of all ownership rights, the method(s) of acquisition must pass legal muster, the transferor of the object(s) must have absolute ownership when making the transfer, and the document of transferal must include a host of rights of possession (e.g., copyright or trademark rights).[158]

Getting these assurances is not always easy, but it is nonetheless a burden museums bear in agreeing to accept collections and being able to use them in a variety of ways. How did the transferor come into possession of the object(s)? Were legal conventions, laws, and regulations followed in obtaining the object(s)? Are there others who may claim partial ownership of the collection? Does the transferor have all rights or only limited rights to the object(s)? These and other questions determine how your museum's deed-of-gift form should be worded. But "there are no substitutes for common sense and a bit of skepticism when accepting objects for the museum, regardless of how carefully drawn the deed of gift may be."[159] Each potential acquisition should be researched, and each potential donor should be questioned, to reveal the history and ownership of the object(s).

Factors Affecting Title

Status of the transferor: The person making the gift should have clear and complete title. The donor should be questioned about other possible owners, such as a spouse, children, siblings, or a business partner; if there are others, clear title can only be given if all other owners sign the deed-of-gift form as well. Inherited gifts should also be investigated, as there are sometimes family and legal disagreements over ownership.

Validity of the gift: If there are questions about the age, authenticity, or legal ownership of the gift (e.g., if the gift turns out to be fake, stolen, or misrepresented to you) there are a few legal remedies (see Marie Malaro's *A Legal Primer on Managing Museum Collections*[160]). Nothing, however, provides as much assurance as careful questioning of the donor, a curatorial review of the gift (by an outside authenticator, if necessary), and a little research.

Legal issues regarding provenance (source or origin of the object): Since the last half of the twentieth century, there has been increasing concern for, and legal attention paid to, objects representing cultural and national heritage. No matter its discipline or size, a museum is subject to the conventions, treaties, laws, statutes, and regulations dealing with these types of objects. If your museum has archeological, artistic, historical, or cultural material from this country or others, or accepts such material, you are bound by such legislation. Table 4.1 provides a brief overview, but for a more in-depth discussion, see Malaro's *A Legal Primer*[161] and Sherry Hutt, Caroline M. Blanco, and Ole Varmer's, *Heritage Resources Law: Protecting the Archeological and Cultural Environment.*[162]

Legal issues regarding plants and wildlife: As with cultural patrimony, federal, state, and some foreign laws are aimed at protecting certain plants and wildlife—even parts of plants and wildlife that may be incorporated into objects collected by museums or sold by museum stores. The laws regulate the disposition, sale, trade, collection, and transportation of certain wildlife and plants, and both live and dead specimens are covered. Along with the federal legislation listed in table 4.2, be sure to check any applicable state and foreign laws that may be relevant to objects you hold or may obtain for collections, research, or your museum store. For a discussion of these types of laws, see Hutt, Blanco, and Varmer's *Heritage Resources Law.*

Illegally imported art: Claims for return of works of art with Nazi-era provenance have increased in recent years, and U.S. law usually favors original owners over so-called good-faith purchasers, such as museums that obtain the works without knowledge of their source. To avoid or mitigate legal trouble, museums should "identify all objects in their collections that were created before 1946 and acquired by the museum after 1932, that underwent a change of ownership between 1932 and 1946, and that were or might reasonably be thought to have been in continental Europe between those dates; make currently available object and provenance (history of ownership) information on those objects accessible; and give priority to continuing provenance research as resources allow."[163] The AAM has been active in working on this issue and providing resources and guidance.[164]

Table 4.1. Legal Issues Regarding Provenance (Source or Origin of the Object)

Legislation	Date	What It Does	Reference
Antiquities Act	1906	Illegal to harm or remove without authorization antiquities located on certain government-controlled property.	• Act[165] • Malaro[166]
Hague Convention for the Protection of Cultural Property in Times of Armed Conflict	1954	Provides guidelines for the protection of museums, archives, and libraries during wartime, and also for artifacts, monuments, archaeological sites, architecture, and other property.	• Convention[167] • Standard Practices Handbook for Museums[168]
UNESCO Convention on the Means of Prohibiting and Preventing the Illicit Import, Export, and Transfer of Ownership of Cultural Property	1970	Addresses concerns about archaeological looting and removal of such objects from their country of origin.	• Malaro[169]
National Historic Preservation Act	1966; 2006	Provides federal protection to prehistoric and historic resources—including sites, districts, buildings, structures, and objects significant in American history, architecture, archaeology, engineering, and culture—through National Register listing.	• Act[170] • Malaro[171]
Archaeological Resources Protection Act	1979	Makes it illegal to sell, purchase, exchange, transport, receive, or offer to sell, purchase, or exchange any archaeological resource if it was excavated or removed from public or Indian lands or in violation of any provision, rule, regulation, ordinance, or permit in effect under state or local law. This includes such items as pottery, basketry, bottles, weapons, weapon projectiles, tools, structures or portions of structures, pit houses, rock paintings, rock carvings, intaglios, graves, human skeletal materials, or any portion or piece thereof.	• Act[172] • Malaro[173]
UNIDROIT Convention on Stolen or Illegally Exported Cultural Objects	1995	Regulates the international movement of cultural property.	• Convention[174] • Malaro[175]
Native American Graves Protection and Repatriation Act	1990	Requires all federal agencies/departments, all state and local governments, and any institution/organization receiving federal funding to inventory and complete summaries of Native American remains and funerary objects, sacred objects, and objects of cultural patrimony in their collections. The data are then provided to Native American individuals, Indian tribes, and native Hawaiian organizations, which in turn identify those remains and objects that were likely culturally affiliated to them. Also delineates the processes for repatriation (return) claims, standards of proof, resolving disputes, and transfer of materials.	• Act[176] • NAGPRA website[177] • King[178] • Malaro[179]
UNESCO Convention on the Protection of the Underwater Heritage	2001	Protects underwater sites and their cultural materials and the conservation and management of recovered underwater heritage.	• Convention[180] • Standard Practices Handbook for Museums[181]

Table 4.2. Legal Issues Regarding Plants and Wildlife

Legislation	Date	What It Does	Reference
Lacey Act	1900	Prohibits the importation, exportation, transportation, sale, receipt, acquisition, or purchase of any fish, wildlife, or plant taken or possessed in violation of any law, treaty, or regulation of the United States or in violation of any Indian tribal law.	• Act[182] • USDA's Animal & Plant Health Inspection Service[183] • Malaro[184]
Migratory Bird Treaty Act	1918	Prohibits the kill, capture, collection, possession, purchase, sale, shipment, import, or export of migratory game and non-game birds, as well as their parts, nests, or eggs, without a federal permit.	• U.S. Fish & Wildlife Service[185] • Malaro[186]
Bald and Golden Eagle Protection Act	1940	Protects bald and golden eagles, along with their parts (e.g., feathers) and products made from them. Exceptions for scientific, exhibition, or Indian religious purposes, but these must be permitted.	• U.S. Fish & Wildlife Service[187] • Malaro[188]
Marine Mammal Protection Act	1972	Protects all marine mammals and prohibits the importation of marine mammals and marine mammal products into the U.S. Exceptions for Indians, Aleuts, or Eskimos who dwell on the coast of the North Pacific Ocean or the Arctic Ocean, and permits may be available for research and display.	• Act[189] • NOAA[190] • Malaro[191]
Convention on International Trade in Endangered Species of Wild Fauna and Flora	1973	Protects living and dead specimens (and their parts and products) of endangered, threatened with extinction, or internally protected species. Species lists are maintained and updated, so continue to check for such species in collections, field collections, and potential donations.	• CITES website[192] • Malaro[193]
Endangered Species Act	1973	Prohibits import, export, sale, trade, or shipment of listed endangered and threatened species, their parts, and products made from them. Some scientific work may be granted permits.	• U.S. Fish & Wildlife Service[194] • Malaro[195]
Antarctic Conservation Act	1978	Prohibits taking native mammals or birds or import of certain Antarctic items into the United States, unless authorized by permit.	• National Science Foundation[196] • Malaro[197]
African Elephant Conservation Act	1988	Prohibits import and export of raw ivory and restricts the movement of worked ivory into and out of the country.	• U.S. Fish & Wildlife Service[198] • Malaro[199]
Wild Bird Conservation Act	1992	Prohibits import of exotic birds in violation of any prohibition, suspension, or quota on importation.	• U.S. Fish & Wildlife Service[200] • Malaro[201]

Gifts

Donor gifts are the primary way most museums acquire collections. A gift is legally made when the donor makes clear his or her intent to make a gift, when the donor actually delivers the gift, and when the gift is accepted by the museum. Unless the donor does not have absolute ownership to make the gift, or unless stipulations regarding ownership are made in documenting the transfer of the gift, the museum receives absolute ownership of the gift.[202]

Restricted gifts are those objects given with strings attached—for example, the stipulation that objects must always be on exhibit or must never be disposed of. While such restrictions may be perfectly legal, they can be, or can become, onerous financially or in terms of use and care. Additionally, "it is difficult to reconcile prudent trusteeship with the acceptance of restrictive conditions that can limit the future usefulness of collection objects or limit the exercise of good judgment by subsequent museum administrators."[203] Short of working with the donor to eliminate such restrictions on a gift, options for deed-of-gift language can mitigate or offset donor restrictions. For more on restricted gifts, see Malaro's *A Legal Primer*.[204]

Depending upon the value of the gift, the IRS has substantiation (value-verification) regulations governing written gift acknowledgments, appraisals, and IRS form completion in order for a donor to receive a tax deduction. Most IRS substantiation rules are triggered by gifts valued at $250 or more. For a detailed discussion of the substantiation and disclosure requirements for gifts, see IRS regulations.[205]

Purchases

Since museum objects are generally classified as personal property, their sale and purchase are regulated by the Uniform Commercial Code (UCC).[206] While this often has little impact on museum purchases, it comes into play if the object is found to be fraudulent or its title is found to be faulty. For more information about museum purchases and the UCC, see Marilyn Phelan's *Museums and the Law* or Malaro's *A Legal Primer*.[207]

A "bargain sale" occurs when an owner offers to sell an object to a museum for less than its fair-market value, thereby gaining a tax advantage for that portion of the object given to the museum. The transaction, then, is partly a sale and partly a charitable contribution. The difficulty arises because the IRS does not have uniform appraisal standards, which means that a donor may declare an object or artwork to be worth much more than its actual value and thereby obtain an inflated charitable deduction. The IRS provides guidance on bargain sales,[208] and museums can take a number of recommended actions to avoid getting drawn into a legal mire.[209]

Field Collection

The legal issues surrounding museums that obtain objects or specimens through field collecting primarily center on permitted and nonpermitted collecting (see "Factors Affecting Title" above for discussions of legal issues regarding provenance and plants and wildlife). The creation of museum policies dealing with national and international laws and conventions on this issue is the best way to proceed so that all those who undertake collecting on the museum's behalf have an understanding of what is and is not permitted by law. "Any field programme must be executed in such a way that all participants act legally and responsibly in acquiring specimens and data, and that they discourage by all practical means unethical, illegal, and destructive practices."[210]

Bequests

Assets left to a museum in someone's will may or may not come as a surprise. Many museums today work with donors to plan for gifts of money or collections upon that donor's death. Upon notification, you should first determine whether an object is appropriate for your mission and collecting priorities, as well as your ability to care for and store it. Bequests do not have to be accepted, or you may decide to take only a portion of the bequest. For more on bequests, see Malaro's *A Legal Primer*.[211]

Loans

Incoming loans: Whenever a loan is arranged, it is paramount that a loan agreement—a written contract detailing the rights and responsibilities of both parties—be created between the museum and the lender. The terms of the agreement prevail should any legal difficulties arise from the loan. Absent the agreement, a bailment situation arises under the law whereby the two parties' rights and responsibilities, as well as the standard of care expected for the object, can put a museum in a dangerous position.[212]

Legal issues for incoming loans also arise around insurance. Without insurance coverage, a museum is assigned the burden of proof that no negligence was involved when, for example, an object is lost or damaged. Coverage by insurance, or acceptance of the lender's insurance, should be detailed in the loan agreement.[213]

The return of loans can also present legal issues for museums. If lenders fail to pick up their property on time, or if a museum cannot find lenders at the loan's end, or if lenders die, the museum is left in the lurch without any control over the property. A well-written loan agreement can help avoid this problem.[214]

Outgoing loans: When a museum is the lender, it wants the best loan conditions possible. Lending to individuals rather than to museums or other organizations can test legal and ethical limits. Additionally, there are legal issues regarding charitable-contribution tax deductions, trustee self-dealing, and the care and protection of objects.[215] Just as for incoming loans, outgoing loans are best insured. If you prefer that the borrower provide insurance, be sure to have documentation, usually a certificate of insurance, before objects leave your museum.[216]

Unclaimed loans: Unclaimed loans—objects whose owners or their whereabouts are unknown or whose owners cannot be contacted—present some of the biggest legal challenges for museums unless your state has a statute for dealing with these situations. The objects lack clear title, so a museum cannot dispose of them and, in fact, may be responsible for storing and caring for them without the authority to do anything else. Expenses to find the owner, or to defend the museum's actions should the owner finally appear once the museum has disposed of the object, may be greater than the museum is able to pay. Three legal doctrines may provide some relief: the statute of limitations, the doctrine of laches, and the notion of adverse possession. To read more about these doctrines, learn more about developments in unclaimed loans, or find out how to research unclaimed loans, see Malaro's *A Legal Primer.*[217]

Objects in temporary custody: Objects brought to the museum for temporary purposes, such as for identification or authentication, incur a different kind of liability in the eyes of the law from those loaned to your museum. Such objects should be documented and signed for when they arrive on what is often called a temporary receipt or temporary custody receipt. Wording on the receipt can explain to the owner, for example, that "although reasonable care will be used, safety is not guaranteed and no insurance will be carried"[218]; this or similar language lets the owner know that the museum is limiting its liability for the objects. Despite this kind of language, you should not let these objects linger at the museum, as expense and liability can accrue despite well-worded receipts. For more about temporary custody procedures, see Malaro's *A Legal Primer.*[219]

Objects "found in the collections": Unclaimed loans aside, many museums have in their collections objects that lack documentation identifying their source, how they came to be in the collections, or when they were added. "In other words, the museum knows that these objects have been in its possession for some time, yet if called on, it cannot prove ownership with certainty because it does not have definitive records."[220] While this may seem a disastrous situation, the law actually puts the burden of proof on a claimant. For more on found objects and how to deal with them, see Malaro's *A Legal Primer.*[221]

Tax Issues

For many people, the benefit of donating collections to a museum is the tax deduction they receive. Generally speaking, such donations to a museum (or another qualified organization), whether of collections or money, are deductible according to IRC 170.[222] The deduction for a collection usually equals its fair-market value at the time of the donation.[223] The IRS defines fair-market value as "the price that property would sell for on the open market; it is the price that would be agreed on between a willing buyer and a willing seller, with neither being required to act, and both having reasonable knowledge of the relevant facts."[224] There are some exceptions to the fair-market rule, however; see Malaro's *A Legal Primer.*[225]

In order for the donor to obtain the deduction, the museum must provide evidence not only that the gift was received by the museum and that the donor relinquished control of it but also that title duly passed to the museum, usually proven by a signed and dated deed-of-gift form. Museums should never back-date museum records, which is considered tax fraud.[226]

A gift given to a museum may not be intended for the museum's collections, or what the IRS considers a "related use" (related to the museum's nonprofit status). Instead, it may be given, for example, to be sold for fundraising, which the IRS considers an "unrelated use," even if the funds raised are used for collection purchases. This distinction is important as related-use gifts provide a more favorable tax advantage. If the gift is intended as an unrelated use, this should be agreed upon by both donor and museum and so noted on the documentation of the gift.[227]

Art Valuation and Appraisals

Appraisals

The issue of museums providing monetary appraisals for donors or prospective donors has raised discussion and legal questions for some time. Since an appraisal is usually sought for tax purposes and a museum is an interested party in the transaction, the self-interest problem for museums was tackled in the Tax Reform Act of 1984. Under that act, a prospective museum donee is not allowed to appraise property that is contributed to the museum over a certain value. Many museums do not provide donors with appraisals as a regular policy, while some, at least under some circumstances, pay for third-party appraisals before the property is donated.[228] As of this writing, appraisals need not be undertaken to receive the tax deduction in certain cases—for example, if the property is worth $500 or less. See Malaro's *A Legal Primer*[229] for other cases.

When donors complete IRS Form 8283, "Noncash Charitable Contributions," for the property they donate, the donee museum is required to sign Part IV, the "Donee Acknowledgment" section. Although the appraised value of the property is included on the form, it clearly states that the museum's signature does not necessarily represent agreement with the claimed fair-market value.[230] However, "if the museum has serious reservations about the value that appears on the form, it should proceed with caution and seek advice from its own tax counsel."[231]

Authenticity

Many museums permit staff members to provide authentications of objects or works of art, in some cases to serve members or others to whom museums cannot provide appraisals. If museum policy states that authentications may be provided, a few areas of possible liability require some degree of caution.

Misrepresentation can be claimed if an assertion about the object is intentionally false or a negligent misstatement, causing foreseeable harm. Providing authentications for free may help lessen liability, but caution is always suggested.[232] Disparagement can be claimed if the authenticator discredits the quality of the object to a third party, which would then interfere with the sale or other use of the object.[233] Defamation can be claimed if a derogatory communication is made that hurts the owner's reputation or association; defamation can be either written (libel) or spoken (slander). For more information, see Malaro's *A Legal Primer*.[234]

Copyright

Museums are both owners and users of intellectual property (IP), which includes all matters of the human mind fixed in tangible form. Examples of IP include copyright on a book or article, a distinctive logo, unique design elements of a website, or a patent on a particular process. IP laws protect, at least temporarily, new or unique products. IP is owned by its creator, who has the right to use, reproduce, or promote it. Four protection categories are covered by IP: copyright, trademarks, patents, and trade secrets. We cover here only copyright, a major issue of concern to museums.[235]

What Is Copyrightable

Copyright is a form of protection provided by law (primarily through the 1976 Copyright Act) to the creators of "original works of authorship," both published and unpublished.[236] These works include literary works; pictorial, graphic, and sculptural works; photographs; audiovisual works; music and sound; and architectural works.[237] Also eligible for copyright protection are certain "derivative works," which are "recast, transformed, or adapted" works based on a preexisting work (e.g., a poster from a photograph, a lithograph based on a painting). Copyright does not protect works not fixed in tangible form (e.g., improvisational speeches); ideas, concepts, and principles; titles, names, short phrases, and slogans; works by the U.S. government; and works of common-property information containing no original authorship.[238]

Owners of copyright have the exclusive right to do, and authorize others to do, the following: reproduce the work; prepare derivative works; distribute copies to the public by sale or other transfer of ownership or by rental, lease, or lending; perform the work publicly; and display the work publicly. These rights, however, have limits, including the doctrine of fair use (see "Fair Use and Other Limitations" below).

Copyright Ownership

Copyright protection exists from the time a work is created in fixed form, and the copyright immediately becomes the property of the work's author. No publication or registration with the U.S. Copyright Office is required to secure copyright, although there are certain advantages to registration. Note that the use of a copyright notice (©) is no longer required under U.S. law.[239] Only the author, or those deriving rights through the author, can claim copyright. For museums, of particular interest are "works made for hire," under which the employer and not the employee is considered the author. Section 101 of the copyright law defines a work made for hire as a work prepared by an employee within the scope of his or her employment or a work specially ordered or commissioned (e.g., a contribution to a collective work or a compilation), if the parties expressly agree in writing signed by them that the work is a work made for hire.[240] Creation of a work by a museum volunteer, even in the context of working for a museum, is likely *not* considered a work for hire; therefore, the copyright resides with the volunteer unless there is a signed, written document transferring copyright.[241] Note especially that mere ownership of a book, manuscript, painting, or any other copy does not give the museum the copyright. The law provides that transfer of ownership of any material object that embodies a protected work does not of itself convey any rights in the copyright.[242] So unless a museum has a signed deed of gift that specifically transfers the copyright of that gift from the copyright owner to the museum, the museum may own the gift but the author, creator, or photographer owns the copyright.

Public Domain

Public domain describes a work that is available to the public and not protected by copyright, due to copyright expiration, failure to renew copyright, or the fact that the work is part of the U.S. government. Some works are specifically tagged as in the public domain. For other works, only research will determine copyright or public-domain status.

Copyright Duration

The term of copyright depends on several factors, including whether a work has been published and, if so, the date of first publication (see tables 4.3 and 4.4).

Table 4.3. When Unpublished and Published Works Pass into the Public Domain in the United States[243]

Unpublished and Unregistered Works		
Type of Work	Copyright Term	What Became Public Domain on 1 January 2010*
Unpublished works	Life of author + 70 years	Works from authors who died before 1940
Unpublished anonymous and pseudonymous works and works made for hire	120 years from date of creation	Works created before 1890
Unpublished works when the death date of author is not known**	120 years from date of creation**	Works created before 1890***

Published Works		
Date of U.S. Publication	Conditions	Copyright Term*
Before 1923	None	In public domain
1923 through 1977	Published without a copyright notice	In public domain
1978 to 1 March 1989	Published without notice and without subsequent registration within five years	In public domain
1978 to 1 March 1989	Published without notice but with subsequent registration within five years	70 years after death of author, or, if work of corporate authorship, the shorter of 95 years from publication or 120 years from creation
1923 through 1963	Published with notice but copyright was not renewed****	In public domain
1923 through 1963	Published with notice and copyright was renewed****	95 years after publication date
1964 through 1977	Published with notice	95 years after publication date
1978 to 1 March 1989	Published with notice	70 years after death of author, or if work of corporate authorship, the shorter of 95 years from publication or 120 years from creation
1978 to 1 March 1989	Created before 1978 and first published with notice in the specified period	The greater of the term specified in the previous entry or 31 December 2047

Published Works

Date of U.S. Publication	Conditions	Copyright Term
From 1 March 1989 through 2002	Created after 1977	70 years after death of author. If a work of corporate authorship, 95 years from publication or 120 years from creation, whichever expires first
From 1 March 1989 through 2002	Created before 1978 and first published in this period	The greater of the term specified in the previous entry or 31 December 2047
After 2002	None	70 years after death of author. If a work of corporate authorship, 95 years from publication or 120 years from creation, whichever expires first
Anytime	Works prepared by an employee of the U.S. government as part of their official duties	None

*All terms of copyright run through the end of the calendar year in which they would otherwise expire, so a work enters the public domain on the first of the year following the expiration of its copyright term. For instance, a book published on March 15, 1923, will enter the public domain on January 1, 2019, not March 16, 2018.

**These works may still be copyrighted, but certification from the U.S. Copyright Office is a complete defense against any action for infringement.

***Presumption of the author's death requires a certified report from the U.S. Copyright Office that its records disclose nothing to indicate that the author of the work is living or died less than seventy years before.

****A 1961 Copyright Office study found that fewer than 15 percent of all registered copyrights were renewed. For textual material (including books), the figure was 7 percent.

Fair Use and Other Limitations

Although the courts have ruled on no real definition of the concept of fair use, U.S. copyright law sets out four factors to be considered in determining whether a particular use of a copyrighted work is fair: the purpose and character of the use (e.g., commercial versus nonprofit educational use), the nature of the copyrighted work (e.g., a fictional versus factually based work), the amount and substantiality of the portion used in relation to the copyrighted work as a whole, and the effect of the use upon the potential market for or value of the copyrighted work.[244]

Under fair use, the copyright law in Section 107 specifically addresses classroom reproductions, particularly photocopying of books and periodicals, in nonprofit educational institutions, both in single copies for teachers (for research and class preparation) and in multiple copies for students (for classroom discussion). These copies have to meet the rules of brevity, spontaneity, and cumulative effect. For details on these uses, see "Reproduction of Copyrighted Works by Educators and Librarians."[245]

Table 4.4. When Sound Recordings Pass into the Public Domain in the United States

Sound Recordings[247]		
Date of Fixation/Publication	Conditions	What Became Public Domain on 1 January 2010**
Unpublished but fixed prior to 15 February 1972	Indeterminate	Subject to state common law protection. Enters the public domain on 15 February 2067
Unpublished but fixed after 15 February 1972	Life of the author + 70 years. For unpublished anonymous and pseudonymous works and works made for hire, 120 years from the date of fixation	Nothing. The soonest anything enters the public domain is 15 February 2067
Fixed prior to 15 February 1972	None	Subject to state statutory and/or common law protection. Fully enters the public domain on 15 February 2067
15 February 1972–1978	Published without notice (i.e., ℗, year of publication, and name of copyright owner)	In the public domain
15 February 1972–1978	Published with notice	95 years from publication; 2068 at the earliest
1978–1 March 1989	Published without notice and without subsequent registration	In the public domain
1978–1 March 1989	Published with notice	70 years after death of author, or if work of corporate authorship, the shorter of 95 years from publication, or 120 years from creation. 2049 at the earliest
After 1 March 1989	None	70 years after death of author, or if work of corporate authorship, the shorter of 95 years from publication, or 120 years from creation. 2049 at the earliest

**These works may still be copyrighted, but certification from the U.S. Copyright Office is a complete defense against any action for infringement.

The copyright law under Section 108 contains some exemptions giving libraries and archives limited reproduction and distribution rights,[246] including making preservation and replacement copies, although the exemptions have to meet certain limits. "Though the copyright law specifically mentions nonprofit libraries and archives, the exemptions in section 108 would seem to apply to museums also and certainly to museum archives and libraries."[248]

The rule known as the first sale doctrine also applies to copyrighted works. Under the Copyright Act, "the owner of a particular copy . . . is entitled, without the authority of the copyright owner, to sell or otherwise dispose of the possession of the copy."[249] A visitor who buys a museum exhibit catalog, for example, may later give it away or resell it, but he or she may not make multiple copies of it for wider distribution.[250] Likewise, should a museum purchase computer software or a copy of a sound recording, it is not allowed to reproduce, rent, or lend it "without the permission of the copyright owner, subject to certain exceptions for nonprofit educational institutions and libraries."[251] Electronic resources like DVDs are generally licensed, not owned, and therefore are not subject to the right of first sale.

Copyright law also applies to public performances, which include lectures, songs, dramatic works, dance, and films performed in a public place, which a museum is considered to be. The composer, playwright, or choreographer generally owns the public performance rights, and most often these are licensed through performing rights organizations (see "Contracts and Licensing Agreements" on pages 89–90 of this book), which then issue licenses to organizations such as museums. For more on this topic, see "Use of Videotapes/DVDs/Video Files."[252]

Liability

Although copyright issues may seem small or inconsequential to the casual "borrower" of copyrighted material, copyright violators now face not just civil but also criminal penalties. Willful copyright infringement, meaning use for financial gain or reproduction or distribution valued at more than $1,000, can incur imprisonment for up to five years and fines of up to $150,000 per infringement.[253]

Copyright Permission

Finding whom you should contact for copyright permission can be a difficult or time-consuming task. If you know the author or publisher, you can contact that person directly. Most websites have a copyright section at the bottom of their pages giving contact information. Otherwise, you can look at various media-based sites. If the work is part of a book or a journal article, try searching for it on the Copyright Clearance Center website.[254] If you are seeking the copyright holder for an image, you can contact a number of professional organizations representing image creators.[255] For musical works, see the organizations listed on page 90 of this book under "Contracts and Licensing Agreements." For permissions for theatrical works, see "Obtaining Rights to Produce a Play or Musical or Use Music in Live Performances."[256] For film rights, contact one of the three motion picture licensing organizations that grant public performance rights.[257] For other tips on obtaining copyright permission, see "Getting Permission."[258]

Oral Histories

An oral history is the product (document, video, audio recording) resulting from a systematic interview of a person or people relaying firsthand knowledge or memories of general or specific events in their lives. There are many legal issues when conducting and using oral histories; the best, detailed resource to assist museums through the process is John A. Neuenschwander's *A Guide to Oral History and the Law*.[259] The Oral History Association (OHA) is another good source for keeping updated on current legal issues in the field.[260]

It is the responsibility of the interviewer to make certain that the interviewee understands his or her rights, including, but not limited to, issues of editing, access, copyright, and the anticipated disposition or dissemination of the interview in all possible formats.[261] In all cases, interviewees own the copyright to their interviews until and unless those rights are transferred to the museum. Interviews should remain confidential until expressed written permission is given to use them.

Rights are usually transferred by way of a signed release form, samples of which are available through Internet searches or by asking other museums for copies of theirs. Neuenschwander includes sample forms in his book.[262]

"The best legal release agreements contain precise but not overly legalistic language, document the full meeting of the minds between the parties on all relevant issues, and provide a road map for future use and administration. In other words, your agreement should be readily explainable to a lay person and defensible in court should such a challenge ever come to pass."[263]

There may be negative consequences surrounding oral histories and release forms, including compelled release of interviews (e.g., subpoenas and FOIA requests), defamation, privacy issues, use of oral histories on the Internet, and whether an interviewer has a duty to report a crime exposed in an interview. For more information, see Neuenschwander's *A Guide to Oral History and the Law*.[264]

If your museum conducts oral history interviews as part of, or on behalf of, a college or university, most require review of your protocols by their institutional review board (IRB), which is charged with protecting the rights and interests of interview subjects. This has been a hot-button issue for some. The OHA suggests that, before conducting an oral history project or dealing with an IRB review, college- or university-affiliated individuals take a reasonable course of action that includes informing themselves of the pertinent federal regulations and taking a proactive approach with the IRB.[265]

Collections and Freedom of Expression

The nature of some objects or artworks in museum collections, whether on exhibit, in program materials, or posted on the Internet, may be seen as obscene, lewd, or indecent by a segment of the public. Laws and standards on this issue vary by state and community, and there are state and federal criminal penalties for providing obscene material to the public.

In general, the area most often of concern is nudity. State and local courts have judged some nudity, particularly in photographs, to be obscene, although educational, medical, or scientific images are less likely to be judged sexually explicit. Images of nude children and of sexually explicit conduct are most likely to draw litigation. An informal advisory panel of scholars, art historians, and visual arts lawyers may be helpful in determining your likelihood of running afoul of local or state standards and may be seen as a good-faith effort should claims be brought against your museum.[266]

Collections Management

Conservation

The care and conservation of objects and artworks in museum collections are ethical obligations and also part of the broad brush of legal duties that are board of trustees' responsibilities, described above under "Governance Responsibilities" as their duty of obedience (see page 83). A prudent board will demand periodic reports on collections care, seek preventive conservation work when possible,[267] and take appropriate action should serious problems arise; otherwise, it will become vulnerable to litigation.[268]

This is a difficult area for small museums, since few can afford to keep a conservator on staff or even to perform regular conservation surveys to keep abreast of the condition of collections. Use of conservation assessments—such as the Conservation Assessment Program, which is funded through a cooperative agreement between the Institute of Museum and Library Services and Heritage Preservation[269]—is one way to attempt to meet this duty.

Insurance

Whether to insure collections is generally an individual museum's decision. Because insurance can be expensive, when it comes to their own collections, some museums instead opt to spend money on security systems and better collections care. Museums that have multiple sites or store collections off-site sometimes prefer the insurance option, although, at best, insurance only pays for claims on lost, damaged, or stolen collections that in most cases are irreplaceable.

Board of trustees' duty of care in exercising reasonable oversight is the primary legal element of insurance. If trustees exercise due diligence in determining the best course of action for protecting collections, legal challenges will likely be minimized. "The law does not require that the board make the 'right' decision (known, of course, only with the benefit of hindsight)—only that the board inform itself and make a reasonable decision based on the information before it."[270]

A different set of circumstances arises for collections not owned by the museum, such as borrowed collections or those temporarily at the museum (e.g., for acquisition consideration). Loan agreements or temporary receipts may contractually necessitate insurance coverage, but it may be wise to insure all non-museum-owned collections to protect against possible claims of negligence. Even if a lender or owner signs a waiver of liability, a museum may still be held liable.[271]

For more information on insurance and what to look for in an insurance policy, see Malaro's *A Legal Primer*.[272]

Disposal

Deaccessioning: Deaccessioning is the formal and scrupulous culling of objects from a museum's collections—because they are duplicates, damaged, or not mission related, for example—and the subsequent disposal of those objects by sale, trade, donation, or destruction. Both the American Association for State and Local History and the American Association of Museums support the ethical rule that proceeds from the disposal of deaccessioned objects may only be used for the purchase of other collections or the direct care and conservation of existing collections and not for other purposes such as budget shortfalls or facility renovations.[273]

Although most deaccessioning issues are primarily ethical at heart, recent well-publicized cases have found their way into the legal system. However, courts "appear to be reluctant to inhibit the discretion of trustees in this area."[274] The main legal sticking point is assuring that the museum holds clear title to objects before they are considered for deaccessioning. Good work on the front end when acquiring objects (i.e., obtaining clear title along with the acquisition) minimizes legal problems when deaccessioning. When clear title is held, your museum is not legally required to obtain donor consent to deaccession.[275] Without clear title, no object should be considered for deaccession, or else you must be prepared to face a legal challenge.

Under the Tax Reform Act of 1984 and IRS regulations relating to it, "the Internal Revenue Code now requires, in some situations, that a museum notify the donor and the Internal Revenue Service if certain donated property ($5,000 for any single item, $5,000 for aggregate of similar items) is sold, exchanged, or otherwise transferred within two years of the date of the gift."[276] As a result, many museums have adopted as part of their deaccession policy that no donated material will be deaccessioned for two years after the date of its acquisition.

Requests for collection returns: Requests by the donor for return of accessioned museum objects can be a sticky legal and ethical problem for a board of trustees. While the inclusion in most collections policies of a prohibition against return of collections that have clear title may seem straightforward enough, "this does not mean that to fulfill its responsibilities, a museum must pursue to the bitter end every possible argument for retention."[277] A board's duty of care means that it must consider every action, its circumstances, and its own trust responsibilities in coming to a prudent decision.

> If the museum, after investigation, really believes it should acquiesce, then it maintains its credibility by doing so in a timely manner. If, on the other hand, investigation convinces the museum that it should deny the claim, a prompt, clear, written refusal is the most efficient way to resolve the matter. The refusal starts a statute of limitations running so that if the requestor fails to press the claim in court with the time allowed by the relevant statute, the claim is therefore barred.[278]

Access and Use

When it comes to access to and use of collections, the real challenge for museums is balancing public needs with preservation of the collections. These issues are usually a matter for policy and ethics rather than the law, but see the National Park Service's *Museum Handbook* for a list of some of the primary provisions that affect access and use.[279]

As for collections records (e.g., deeds of gift, appraisals, conservation records), legal issues surrounding access include privacy and security concerns, freedom of information, and copyright, especially regarding curatorial or other proprietary research information.

Privacy is important for third-party personal information included in museum records, such as contact information and Social Security numbers. The Federal Privacy Act[280] discusses specific information that cannot be released without the subject's consent and provides procedures for those who can seek access to such records. For a discussion of the kinds of records that fall under privacy laws, see Menzi Behrnd-Klodt's *Navigating Legal Issues in Archives*.[281]

Security concerns for collection records include those that list price and valuation of objects and artworks, such as insurance records and loan agreements. Even access to a museum's architectural records could compromise security. Archeological site maps and documents detailing the whereabouts of endangered species or wildlife could provide sensitive information if free access is allowed.[282]

Both federal and state governments have Freedom of Information statutes that require the release of certain public records. The federal Freedom of Information Act[283] discusses the types of records that are exempt from public disclosure, but these are "topics that do not, as a rule, cover material normally found in museum collection records."[284]

For a chart detailing access and use legal action, see the National Park Service's *Museum Handbook*.[285]

Audiences and the Law

Admission Fees and Tickets

Admission tickets and fees are considered "revocable licenses." A museum can therefore deny visitors admission or have them removed for not complying with museum rules, for inappropriate behavior, or for submitting fraudulent or suspect tickets. Refunds and exchanges are usually prohibited.[286] Museum rules and sometimes the conditions for revocation are printed directly on a ticket and are sometimes detailed on a museum's website. Some museums include within their rules that tickets cannot be purchased from a third party (e.g., a ticket broker or a scalper).

Membership

Membership dues are considered by the IRS to be charitable contributions if your museum is a qualified nonprofit organization. While such contributions are tax deductible as allowed by law, if members receive a benefit from their contribution, deductibility is limited to the amount of the contribution that is more than the value of the benefit received. Both the museum and the member can disregard certain membership benefits in return for an annual payment of $75 or less. For more on dues deductibility, see IRS Publication 526.[287] For more on your museum's duty to furnish information to donors and for substantiation of contributions, see Barry Szczesny, "Are Museum Memberships Tax Deductible?"[288]

Some museums sell their membership lists to other museums, nonprofits, or businesses whose services might be of interest to members. Sale of your membership list is a matter of member privacy, so it may be a good idea to allow members the chance to opt out of the list you sell.[289]

Accessibility

All museums have a legal responsibility to make their facilities, programs, and exhibits accessible to persons with disabilities. The Americans with Disabilities Act of 1990 (ADA)[290] is the federal civil rights law that prohibits exclusion of people with disabilities. The law is applicable to employment, governmental activities, public accommodations, and, since 1996, telecommunications.[291]

Under ADA, "disability" refers to physical or mental impairment that substantially limits a person in some major life activities; this includes someone who has a record of such an impairment as well as someone who is regarded as having such an impairment. Importantly, impairments are not limited solely to mobility, visual, or hearing impairments; they also include conditions such as epilepsy, heart disease, mental impairments, emotional illness, and drug or alcohol addiction.[292] "Quite simply, the ADA asks a museum to think creatively not only about ways to bring more disabled people into its facilities but also about ways to provide those who come with all reasonable means to participate in programs and activities."[293] For a general approach to accessibility, see chapter 4 in Book 4 of this series.

The most common concern regarding ADA and museums deals with facilities. All new construction, including parking lots, walkways, and gardens, as well as all changes to existing facilities (remodeling, renovation, rehabilitation, restoration, and reconstruction), must meet ADA guidelines. Since many small museums are housed in historic buildings or have historic outbuildings, accessibility is a major issue. The Department of Justice's guidance on historic buildings states that "if removing barriers or accommodating an activity or program would threaten or destroy the historic significance of a building, the action will not be considered 'readily achievable.' At that point, alternative methods that are readily achievable need to be considered."[294] Existing nonhistoric structures also are required to be accessible when this is "readily achievable," meaning that it can be accomplished without much difficulty or expense. However, "if the museum determines that the removal of a barrier is not readily achievable, it has an obligation to provide an alternative method of accommodation if an alternative is readily achievable."[295] Alternative methods may include such procedures as providing photos or video of second-floor rooms in a historic house without an elevator or offering use of a nonpublic entrance for buildings without easily altered public entrances. See Thomas Jester and Sharon Park, "Making Historic Properties Accessible," for more information.[296]

Along with facility concerns, ADA comes into play in the accessibility of museum programs or activities to those with disabilities. Issues include such options as copies of large-print text labels, Braille labels, or hands-on reproductions of exhibit artifacts or artworks for those with visual impairments; audio-to-print signage, text-telephone machines, captioning, or amplified sound for those with hearing impairments; alternative scripts, labels, or audio for those with mental impairments; and the availability of wheelchairs, canes, or exhibit-hall seating for those with mobility impairments.

For an overview, legal summaries, key requirements, and best practices associated with the ADA, see the National Assembly of State Arts Agencies' *Design for Accessibility: A Cultural Administrator's Handbook.*[297] For assistance with ADA compliance, contact the U.S. Department of Justice.[298] For technical assistance from your state, check the State Code Contact List.[299]

Websites

Multiple legal issues arise when a museum has an online presence. Occasional review of these issues, called "website audits" by Geoffrey Gussis,[300] are warranted to minimize liability. Additionally, insurance policies are now available to cover much of your online liability.

If a third-party website design company develops and maintains your website, you need a written agreement with work-for-hire language; otherwise, the U.S. Copyright Act assigns ownership to the third party. You may consider adding to each webpage a "terms of service" agreement describing allowed and disallowed uses. That section is often accompanied by a privacy policy. Along with adding copyright notices for all museum-owned website materials, you should take care to ascertain that any posted third-party material is either fair use or properly licensed. Likewise, you should check all external links to confirm you are not violating the linking policies of third-party sites.[301]

Privacy

A broad right of privacy is constitutionally protected.[302] Many museums, therefore, have privacy policies that provide information to the user, visitor, museum member, or others regarding their rights to privacy.

A website's terms of service may state what nonpersonal information (e.g., IP address, date and time of visit) as well as what personal information (e.g., name, e-mail address) it does or does not automatically collect from its users. A privacy policy often states what information the museum will share with or sell to third parties, options for accepting or rejecting cookies (small pieces of data sent to your Web browser to assist with your use of the site), and possible disclosure to law enforcement. Such a policy often includes an explanation of how the website owner protects confidentiality and security. Because museums often deal with young children, many privacy policies specifically include language about the Children's Online Privacy Protection Act,[303] which restricts the use and disclosure of the personal information of children age twelve or younger.

A privacy policy may discuss how your museum ensures that credit card transactions are secure and how you use data collected from surveys. It may detail how your museum uses private information gathered on a website, from visitors, during a museum store transaction, or from a membership purchase.

Museums frequently use photographs, film, audio, and the like, taken of participants during museum programs, activities, and special events, for publicity, websites, and marketing. Since museums are usually classified as public places where the public is invited, there is no expectation of privacy, and photographs taken there generally are not actionable.[304] However, it is worth studying ways to avoid possible lawsuits.[305] Obtaining a signed release to use a person's name or image can be important since, if that person feels his or her privacy has been invaded, he or she can sue the museum for monetary damages. Such releases must be signed by a parent or guardian if the subject is a minor. Additional protections may apply, however, if the use of the photograph, film, audio, and so forth, is intended for commercial purposes (e.g., for sale or to endorse a product).[306]

Facilities and Risk Management

Risk Management

Risk management is a process to identify, analyze, and take steps to reduce or eliminate exposures to liability. It is impossible to eliminate or even reduce all risk, but "most cases are decided using the 'reasonable man' principle—organizations which take steps a reasonable man would be expected to take to reduce . . . risk are usually found not liable for negligence."[307]

The first step in analyzing your museum's risk is to conduct a tour of the museum, inside and out, and assess its condition and areas of possible risk, not just to visitors but to staff, volunteers, and board members as well. Examples of what to look at include such areas as sidewalks and trails, slip-and-fall locations, wiring, hazardous materials storage, tools and equipment, and hanging branches. Another way to analyze your risk is to use the Nonprofit Risk Management Center's online Nonprofit CARES, a risk management tool designed specifically for nonprofits.[308] The center also offers online tutorials on risk management, volunteers and risk management, and accident prevention and response, along with information about federal and state liability laws.[309] Another source for online assistance dealing with risk management issues is "Risk Identification and Analysis: A Guide for Small Public Entities," which includes sections on identifying and reducing the impact of risks.[310]

Along with brick-and-mortar issues, risk management also applies to the legal and internal control elements of the museum. How is money handled? How do employees know what safety procedures to use? How are statistics and reports created? How are you protected from fraud? The above-named assistance tools can help in this area as well. For more information on identifying fraud and how to deal with it, see Melanie Lockwood Herman's "Preventing and Responding to Fraud and Misuse of Assets in a Nonprofit Organization."[311]

Most museum activities and programs in which visitors take part have a low degree of risk, but some may have a higher-than-average risk of injury, such as those involving interactions with animals, fire, hazardous chemicals, or sharp tools. A smart policy is to have participants in these activities sign a waiver of liability before taking part.[312]

Security

Museum security is a wide-ranging issue that covers physical security (e.g., buildings, other facilities, equipment and systems, environmental controls, roadway and vehicle maintenance) and personal security (e.g., safety, accident prevention, emergency training). Security threats and danger come from a wide range of sources, such as vandalism, disasters and emergencies, theft, violent or threatening visitors, environmental accidents, trespassing, weather incidents, construction, waste hazards, infestation, and even terrorism. The keys to eliminating or mitigating such threats are foresight, preparation, knowledge, and training.

A policy that deals with each issue particular to your museum, that deals with risks and anticipates responses, when accompanied by regular staff and volunteer training and practice, is the best way to prepare for the worst. Although training can overcome many threats, a museum also needs systems in place to guard against security problems, such as smoke and fire detectors, response systems, locks, codes, guards, insurance, and disaster-response plans. "Protection is the encompassing system of policies, procedures and physical design that reduces risk and dictates the parameters of any response."[313]

To help in analyzing security risks, the American Society for Industrial Security has online guidelines for a "General Security Risk Assessment." To help bring an institution up to par, there are recommended protection practices listed by the Museum, Library, and Cultural Properties Council of ASIS International and the Museum Association Security Committee of AAM.[314] For more information on improving safety and security, see chapter 1 in Book 3 of this series.

The legal issues surrounding museum security primarily have to do with liability. "Whether a museum's security procedures fall so short of accepted professional standards as to constitute a violation of legal responsibilities depends on the facts of a particular situation. But if little thought has been given to security, a museum is placing itself in a vulnerable position."[315]

Health and Safety

Keeping a healthy and safe working environment for employees and volunteers and a healthy and safe venue for visitors is one more way to avoid legal action directed at a museum. The Occupational Safety and Health Act of 1970,[316] administered by the Department of Labor's Occupational Safety and Health Administration (OSHA), assures safe and healthful working conditions for workers and provides information, education, and training in the occupational safety and health field. In addition to the requirements to comply with the regulations and safety and health standards contained in the act, employers have a general duty to provide a workplace free from serious hazards.

One or more agencies in each state are authorized to implement federal safety and health requirements. Therefore, both OSHA and the appropriate state agency, as well as local code-compliance officials (fire, safety, and building codes), are resources when requesting help in identifying safety and health hazards. Identifying hazards not only helps avoid employee injury claims but also provides a safer environment for visitors. After you identify hazards and make changes, requesting an audit from a local fire or police department can provide additional buffering against liability claims. The "reasonable man" principle mentioned under "Risk Management" above also applies to health and safety concerns.

A few health and safety issues deserve special mention. Every workplace that deals with chemicals should maintain and make available to its employees a central file of material safety data sheets (MSDSs). An MSDS is a detailed informational document prepared by the manufacturer of a hazardous chemical that describes the physical and chemical properties of the product. There are many MSDS search sites online to help in researching chemicals; many are indexed at Kansas State University's James R. MacDonald Laboratory site.[317]

A museum's collections can be a source of health and safety issues due to artifacts with pesticide residues (arsenic, DDT, mercury compounds) and pigments (lead, mercury, uranium), as well as conservation supplies like solvents, pesticides, fumigants, and preservatives.[318] Other locations of potentially hazardous materials are exhibit construction areas (paints, laminates, adhesives), historic buildings (lead-based paint and asbestos), buildings and grounds areas (pesticides, paints, gasoline, cleaning supplies), office supply storage areas (photocopy chemicals), and darkrooms (photo chemicals). Trained health experts can help identify hazardous materials and recommend procedures to reduce the health and safety risks.[319]

The Federal Insecticide, Fungicide, and Rodenticide Act (FIFRA)[320] provides federal control of pesticide distribution, sale, and use. Because pests can cause such damage, most importantly to museum collections, and because museum lawns and grounds are often the play areas for children, FIFRA can play a major role in help-ing to reduce calls for legal action.

Emergencies and Disasters

Despite well-publicized cases of disasters at museum across the country—ranging from floods and fires to hurricanes and tornadoes—a majority of mu-seums, especially small and midsized ones, still lack emergency and disaster plans. "When a duty of care is imposed on an organization, those who govern the organization are responsible for protecting against reasonably foreseeable dangers. If a particular danger frequently has catastrophic effects, the respon-sibility to protect is heightened. . . . From a legal point of view, a museum has little excuse not to give a reasonable amount of attention to such planning."[321] The AAM provides a plethora of resources for developing disaster plans,[322] along with a wealth of materials for emergency preparedness and recovery.[323] Additional resources on disaster planning are listed in chapter 1 of Book 3 of this series.

Museum boards are ultimately responsible for their museum's ability to pre-pare for and respond to disasters and emergencies. Therefore, consideration of the issues, policy development, planning, and review constitute a reasonable course of action. "If decision-makers take the time to inform themselves, reach an agree-ment, and make a record of the process, the chances are quite good that their deci-sion not only will be a sensible one but also will withstand any legal challenge."[324]

National Register Buildings

If a museum owns or is housed in buildings that are on the National Regis-ter of Historic Places or are of National Register quality, their maintenance and repair are affected by historic preservation laws, most prominently the National Historic Preservation Act of 1966 and later amendments.[325] Any modification to such a building must follow Department of Interior regulations to stay on the National Register. The most recent regulations are referred to in "The Secretary of the Interior's Standards for the Treatment of Historic Properties," which provides standards for preservation, rehabilitation, restoration, and reconstruc-tion, as well as sources for technical information.[326] To help offset the costs of maintaining National Register buildings, the Federal Historic Preservation Tax Incentives program offers a 20 percent tax credit for the rehabilitation of income-producing historic structures.[327]

Construction and Renovation

The major legal issue surrounding construction or renovation of buildings involves code compliance. The International Code Council has developed a national building code.[328] Additional requirements for existing buildings can be found on the National Fire Protection Association's website,[329] where codes dealing with historic buildings can also be found.[330]

Code compliance is a particularly difficult issue when dealing with historic buildings constructed of materials and in configurations that differ from the requirements of new construction. "Historic preservation is neither the primary mission of code officials nor a value reflected in most code documents. Even if supportive of preservation, the code official is often granted limited discretion by the regulations to vary from the code. The code official may also be concerned with the precedent-setting implications of each decision and personal-liability exposure, an anxiety fed by the litigious construction climate."[331] Boards of historic houses and museums housed in historic structures that are dealing with these legal difficulties are encouraged to work with their state and, if necessary, federal historic preservation organizations.

Miscellaneous Facility-Related Regulations

State laws regulating such equipment as elevators, platform lifts, and escalators vary by state. "States regulate elevators to prevent the use of unsafe and defective lifting devices, which impose a substantial probability of serious and preventable injury to employees and the public exposed to unsafe conditions."[332] For more about elevator codes and standards, see the National Elevator Industry's website.[333]

Museums' outside signs and banners are subject to sign ordinances, which come under the aegis of city regulations.

For museums that fly the U.S. flag, the laws relating to the flag are found in detail in the United States Code.[334]

Selected Bibliography

Adams-Graf, Diane, and Claudia J. Nicholson. "Thinking Ahead about Museum Protection: An Ounce of Prevention Is Worth a Pound of Cure." Minnesota Historical Society, *Tech Talk*, 2000. www.mnhs.org/about/publications/techtalk/TechTalkMarch2000.pdf.

Alberta Museums Association. *Standard Practices Handbook for Museums*. Museum Excellence Series 1. 2nd ed. Edmonton, Alberta: Alberta Museums Association, 1990.

Behrnd-Klodt, Menzi L. *Navigating Legal Issues in Archives*. Chicago: Society of American Archivists, 2008.

Bruwelheide, Janis H. *The Copyright Primer for Librarians and Educators*. 2nd ed. Chicago: American Library Association, 1995.

Buck, Rebecca A., and Jean Allman Gilmore, eds. *The New Museum Registration Methods*. 4th ed. Washington, DC: American Association of Museums, 1998.

Crimm, Walter L., Martha Morris, and L. Carole Wharton. *Planning Successful Museum Building Projects*. Walnut Creek, CA: AltaMira Press, 2009.

Duerksen, Christopher J., ed. *A Handbook on Historic Preservation Law*. Washington, DC: Conservation Foundation and the National Center for Preservation Law, 1983.

Hopkins, Bruce R. *Legal Responsibilities of Nonprofit Boards*. 2nd ed. Washington, DC: BoardSource, 2009.

Howie, F. Ed. *Safety in Museums and Galleries*. Boston: Butterworths, 1987.

Hurwit, Jeffrey. "Nonprofit Governance: An Introduction to Current Legal & Ethical Issues." Hurwit & Associates, 2005. www.hurwitassociates.com/NEMA-2005.pdf.

Hutt, Sherry, and David Tarler, eds. *Yearbook of Cultural Property Law 2009*. Walnut Creek, CA: Left Coast Press, 2009.

King, Thomas F. *Cultural Resource Laws & Practice: An Introductory Guide*. 2nd ed. Walnut Creek, CA: AltaMira Press, 2004.

Koelling, Jill Marie. *Digital Imaging: A Practical Approach*. Walnut Creek, CA: AltaMira Press, 2004.

Kuyper, Joan. *Volunteer Program Administration: A Handbook for Museums and Other Cultural Institutions*. New York: American Council for the Arts in Association with the American Association for Museum Volunteers, 1993.

Lind, Robert C., Robert M. Jarvis, and Marilyn E. Phelan. *Art and Museum Law: Cases and Materials*. Durham, NC: Carolina Academic Press, 2002. www.cap-press.com/pdf/1198.pdf.

Liston, David, ed. *Museum Security and Protection: A Handbook for Cultural Heritage Institutions*. New York: International Council of Museums and the International Committee on Museum Security, 1993.

Malaro, Marie C. *A Legal Primer on Managing Museum Collections*. 2nd ed. Washington, DC: Smithsonian Institution Press, 1998.

Merritt, Elizabeth E., ed. *Covering Your Assets: Facilities and Risk Management in Museums*. Washington, DC: American Association of Museums, 2005.

Merryman, John Henry. *Law, Ethics, and the Visual Arts*. Philadelphia: University of Pennsylvania Press, 1987.

National Park Service (NPS). "Legal Issues." In *Museum Handbook*. NPS. www.nps.gov/history/museum/publications/MHIII/mh3ch2.pdf.

Neuenschwander, John A. *A Guide to Oral History and the Law*. New York: Oxford University Press, 2009.

Phelan, Marilyn. *Museums and the Law*. Nashville, TN: AASLH, 1982.

Shapiro, Michael S., and Brett I. Miller. *A Museum Guide to Copyright and Trademark*. Washington, DC: American Association of Museums, 1999.

Skramstad, Harold, and Susan Skramstad. *A Handbook for Museum Trustees*. Washington, DC: American Association of Museums/Museum Trustee Association, 2003.

Urice, Stephen K. "A Contract Law Primer for the Museum Administrator." Paper delivered at the 1999 ALI-ABA Legal Issues in Museum Administration seminar. www.aam-us.org/museumresources/ic/hr/cs/loader.cfm?url=/commonspot/security/getfile.cfm&PageID=2078.

U.S. Copyright Office. "Copyright Basics." U.S. Copyright Office. www.copyright.gov/circs/circ1.pdf.

Wythe, Deborah, ed. *Museum Archives: An Introduction*. 2nd ed. Chicago: Society of American Archivists, 2004.

Yeide, Nancy H., Konstantin Akinsha, and Amy L. Walsh. *The AAM Guide to Provenance Research*. Washington, DC: American Association of Museums, 2001. www.museum-security.org/AAM-provenance.htm.

Notes

1. Marie C. Malaro, *A Legal Primer on Managing Museum Collections*, 2nd ed. (Washington, DC: Smithsonian Institution Press, 1998), 4–10; Marilyn Phelan, *Museums and the Law* (Nashville: American Association for State and Local History, 1982), 1–7.

2. Malaro, *A Legal Primer*, 9–10.

3. Phelan, *Museums and the Law*, 8, 269, and note 1 of chapter 2.

4. Malaro, *A Legal Primer*, 4–10.

5. Phelan, *Museums and the Law*, 30–39.

6. Sherry Butcher-Younghans, *Historic House Museums* (New York: Oxford University Press, 1993), 12.

7. Phelan, *Museums and the Law*, 9.

8. Gerald George and Cindy Sherrell-Leo, *Starting Right*, 2nd ed. (Walnut Creek, CA: AltaMira Press, 2004), 81.

9. Phelan, *Museums and the Law*, 10–12.

10. "Stay Exempt: Tax Basics for Exempt Organizations," Internal Revenue Service, www.stayexempt.irs.gov.

11. A museum with unrelated business income of about $1,000 must file Form 990-T and pay tax on that income. Private foundation museums must file Form 990-PF and pay an excise tax on their net investment income, as well as submit details about activities for the year. Phelan, *Museums and the Law*, 8.

12. "FAQs about the Exempt Organization Public Disclosure Requirements," Internal Revenue Service, www.irs.gov/charities/article/0,,id=96430,00.html.

13. Peter Swords, "How to Read the IRS Form 990 & Find Out What It Means," Nonprofit Coordinating Committee of New York, 2006, www.npccny.org/Form_990/990.htm.

14. Urban Institute, "Form 990," Form 990 Online, http://efile.form990.org.

15. Malaro, *A Legal Primer*, 15. Malaro cites the 1974 Sibley Hospital case, which "is considered a landmark decision and is frequently cited on the issue of nonprofit board member liability" (Malaro, *A Legal Primer*, 11).

16. Malaro, *A Legal Primer*, 19.

17. Malaro, *A Legal Primer*, 19–31; Maureen K. Robinson, *Nonprofit Boards That Work* (New York: John Wiley & Sons, 2001), 31–35.

18. "Developing an Institutional Code of Ethics," American Association of Museums, www.aam-us.org/museumresources/ic/gso/ae/institutional.cfm.

19. Robinson, *Nonprofit Boards That Work*, 13.

20. Richard T. Ingram, *Ten Basic Responsibilities of Nonprofit Boards* (Washington, DC: BoardSource, 2003), 9.

21. Jon Pratt, "Financial Malfeasance and Nonfeasance: Ten Pitfalls Boards Should Avoid," Minnesota Council of Nonprofits, www.mncn.org/info/basic_fin.htm#financial malfeasance and nonfeasance.

22. Phelan, *Museums and the Law*, 154.

23. "Insurability Checklist," American Association of Museums, www.aam.npo-ins .com/rm_checklist.jsp?subd=aam.

24. "Protecting Your Nonprofit and the Board," Nonprofit Risk Management Center, www.nonprofitrisk.org/library/articles/insurance0101999.shtml.

25. Elaine L. Johnston and Annemarie Thomas, "Nuts and Bolts of Insurance: Directors and Officers Liability and Media Liability," American Association of Museums, www.aam-us.org/museumresources/ic/frm/rm/loader.cfm?url=/commonspot/security/getfile.cfm&PageID=2443.

26. Jeffrey Hurwit, "Nonprofit Governance: An Introduction to Current Legal & Ethical Issues," Hurwit & Associates, www.hurwitassociates.com/NEMA-2005.pdf.

27. Knowledge Center Q&A, "Can Minors Serve on Boards?" BoardSource, www .boardsource.org/Knowledge.asp?ID=3.103.

28. Jason Hall, "Nonprofits and Government: What You Can and Can't Do," American Association of Museums, March 2006, www.speakupformuseums.org/docs/Rules%20of%20Nonprofit%20Lobbying.pdf.

29. "FCC Freedom of Information Act (FOIA)," Federal Communications Commission, www.fcc.gov/foia.

30. "Guide to the Freedom of Information Act (2009 Edition)," U.S. Department of Justice, www.justice.gov/oip/foia_guide09.htm.

31. "Your Right to Federal Records," General Services Administration, www.pueblo .gsa.gov/cic_text/fed_prog/foia/foia.htm.

32. "Insurability Checklist," American Association of Museums, www.aam.npo-ins .com/rm_checklist.jsp?subd=aam.

33. "Friends & Foundations Fact Sheets," Association of Library Trustees, Advocates, Friends, and Foundations, www.ala.org/ala/mgrps/divs/altaff/friends/factsheets/index.cfm.

34. "Code of Ethics for Museums Friends and Volunteers," World Federation of Friends of Museums, www.museumsfriends.com/codeofethics.asp.

35. "Charitable Support Tax Exempt Organizations," Thompson and Thompson, www.t-tlaw.com/lr-08.htm.

36. See GiftLaw Pro at www.giftlaw.com/glaw_giftlawpro.jsp.

37. "Museum Retailing—UBIT Issues," Internal Revenue Service, www.irs.gov/pub/irs-tege/eotopicu79.pdf.

38. Jeffrey Hurwit, "The Entrepreneurial Museum: Some Legal, Tax, and Practical Perspectives," Hurwit & Associates, www.hurwitassociates.com/l_entrepreneur_museum.php.

39. "Unrelated Trade or Business," Internal Revenue Service, www.irs.gov/publications/p598/ch03.html.

40. Hurwit, "Nonprofit Governance."

41. Jim Bloom, "IRS Refines Its Position on Museum UBIT Sales of Inventory," Free Library, April 1996, www.thefreelibrary.com/IRS+refines+its+position+on+museum+UBIT+sales+of+inventory.-a018202846.

42. Bloom, "IRS Refines Its Position."

43. Laura Damerville, "BIT Focus: Museum Store Products," *Art Law Clinic Client Newsletter* 1, no. 1 (fall 2005), www.law.harvard.edu/academics/clinical/lsc/pdf/Art%20Law%20Clinic%20Newsletter1.pdf.

44. Damerville, "BIT Focus."

45. "Frequently Asked Advertising Questions: A Guide for Small Business," Federal Trade Commission, www.ftc.gov/bcp/edu/pubs/business/adv/bus35.shtm.

46. Aaron Turpen, "Preventing Fraud on Your Web Site," Museum Store Association, http://nctri.com/anti_fraud.html.

47. Debbie Babcock, "Don't Stand in Line—Buy On-line! Developing and Implementing an E-Commerce Site That Works," Archives & Museum Informatics, 2004, www.archimuse.com/mw2004/papers/babcock/babcock.html.

48. Bloom, "IRS Refines Its Position."

49. Jeffrey Hurwit, "Candlelight, a Glass of Wine, and UBIT: A Food and Facilities Primer," Hurwit & Associates, www.hurwitassociates.com/l_unrelated_candlelight.php.

50. Hurwit, "Candlelight."

51. Hurwit, "Candlelight."

52. "FDA Food Code," U.S. Food and Drug Administration, www.fda.gov/Food/FoodSafety/RetailFoodProtection/FoodCode/default.htm.

53. "Retail Food Protection," U.S. Food and Drug Administration, www.fda.gov/Food/FoodSafety/RetailFoodProtection/default.htm.

54. "Museum Retailing—UBIT Issues," Internal Revenue Service, www.irs.gov/pub/irs-tege/eotopicu79.pdf.

55. Susan Ruth and Charles Barrett, "UBIT: Current Developments," IRS, www.irs.ustreas.gov/pub/irs-utl/topicn.pdf.

56. "What Foundations Need to Know about Federal Funds Management," Council on Foundations, http://ppp.cof.org/cms/wp-content/uploads/2010/06/foundations-fed-funds.pdf; and "Financial Management Guide for Non-Profit Organizations," National Endowment for the Arts, Sept. 2008, http://www.nea.gov/about/oig/fmgnpo.pdf.

57. Lodestar Center for Philanthropy and Nonprofit Innovation, "FAQ: Governance and Boardsmanship," Arizona State University, www.asu.edu/copp/nonprofit/asst/asst_ask_faq_governance.htm.

58. Jeanne Bell and Steve Zimmerman, "Absent the Audit: How Small Nonprofits Can Demonstrate Accountability Without One," The Nonprofit Quarterly (Spring 2007).

59. Lodestar Center, "FAQ: Governance and Boardsmanship."

60. "Statement of Standards," Governmental Accounting Standards Board, http://gasbpubs.stores.yahoo.net/publications-statements-of-standards.html.

61. "Plain Language Documents," Governmental Accounting Standards Board, www.gasb.org/tech/index.html.

62. "Facts about FASB," Financial Accounting Standards Board, www.fasb.org/jsp/FASB/Page/SectionPage&cid=1176154526495.

63. "FASB Accounting Standards Codification," Financial Accounting Standards Board, www.fasb.org/store/subscriptions/fasb/new.

64. "Audit Guide for Small Nonprofit Organizations," Virginia Society of Certified Public Accountants, www.vscpa.com/Visitors/Nonprofit_Resources/Audit_Guide.aspx.

65. Ernie Paszkiewicz, "New Auditing Standards and How They May Impact Your Organization," Standards for Excellence Institute, www.standardsforexcellenceinstitute.org/NewAuditingStandards.html.

66. Carol Norris Vincent, "Creating and Building Endowments for Small Museums," Indiana Historical Society, http://www.indianahistory.org/our-services/local-history-services/CreatingAndBuildingEndowments.pdf.

67. Malaro, *A Legal Primer*, 36–41 and footnotes.

68. Hurwit, "Nonprofit Governance."

69. Stephen K. Urice, "A Contract Law Primer for the Museum Administrator" (paper delivered at the 1999 ALI-ABA Legal Issues in Museum Administration seminar), American Association of Museums, www.aam-us.org/museumresources/ic/hr/cs/loader.cfm?url=/commonspot/security/getfile.cfm&PageID=2078. (You must be logged in to the website to see this paper.)

70. Phil Rabinowitz, "Understanding and Writing Contracts and Memoranda of Agreement," Community Toolbox, 2010, http://ctb.ku.edu/tools/en/sub_section_main_1873.htm.

71. "Planning a Museum Food Service Operation," American Association of Museums, www.aam-us.org/museumresources/ic/fs/ei/loader.cfm?url=/commonspot/security/getfile.cfm&PageID=19253.

72. Joshua Kaufman, "Museum Licensing: How to Do It Right!" American Association of Museums, www.aam-us.org/museumresources/ic/fs/ei/loader.cfm?url=/commonspot/security/getfile.cfm&PageID=7927.

73. Phelan, *Museums and the Law*, 76.

74. "A Canadian Museum's Guide to Developing a Licensing Strategy," Canadian Heritage Information Network, www.pro.rcip-chin.gc.ca/propriete_intellectuelle-intellectual_property/guide_elaboration-guide_developing/index-eng.jsp.

75. American Association of Museums, "Music Licensing for Museums," Museum Store Association, www.museumdistrict.com/resources/AAM_Music_Licensing.pdf.

76. "PCI Quick Reference Guide: Understanding the Payment Card Industry," PCI Security Standards Council, www.pcisecuritystandards.org/pdfs/pci_ssc_quick_guide.pdf.

77. James Hussher, "Credit Card Acceptance for Non-Profit Organizations," Credit Cards Merchant Account, 2009, www.creditcardsmerchantaccount.info/?p=17.

78. Andrew Conry-Murray, "Laws for Organizations That Accept Online Payments," TechSoup, www.techsoup.org/learningcenter/webbuilding/page6432.cfm.

79. "Charitable Solicitation—State Requirements," Internal Revenue Service, www.irs .gov/charities/charitable/article/0,,id=123045,00.html; Karl E. Emerson, "State Charitable Solicitation Statutes," Internal Revenue Service, www.irs.gov/pub/irs-tege/ eotopici01.pdf.

80. "U.S. Charity Offices," National Association of State Charity Officials, www .nasconet.org/agencies.

81. "Fundraising: What Laws Apply?" Guidestar, www.2.guidestar.org/rxa/news/ articles/2003/fundraising-what-laws-apply.aspx?articleId=864.

82. The National Association of Attorneys General maintains contact information for the attorney general in each state; see the National Association of State Charity Officials.

83. Guidestar, "Fundraising: What Laws Apply?"

84. Internal Revenue Service, "Taxation of Tax-Exempt Organizations' Income from Corporate Sponsorship," GPO Access, http://frwebgate.access.gpo.gov/cgi-bin/getdoc .cgi?dbname=2002_register&docid=02-9930-filed.pdf.

85. Lindsay Bleier, "'Tis the Season for Corporate Sponsorship," *Art Law Clinic Client Newsletter* 1, no. 1 (fall 2005): 6–8, www.law.harvard.edu/academics/clinical/lsc/pdf/ Art%20Law%20Clinic%20Newsletter1.pdf.

86. Bleier, "'Tis the Season."

87. Bleier, "'Tis the Season."

88. Judith Barker, "Legal Issues in Sponsorship: Get It in Writing," Charity Village, www.charityvillage.com/cv/research/rspon10.html.

89. Bleier, "'Tis the Season."

90. Leslie Morgan, "Facts about Institutional Property Tax Exemptions," Shasta County, www.co.shasta.ca.us/html/Assessor/docs/Pamphlets/InstPropTaxExems Pamphlet.pdf.

91. "CERCLA Overview," U.S. Environmental Protection Agency, http://epa.gov/ superfund/policy/cercla.htm.

92. Kathryn W. Miree, "Understanding and Drafting Nonprofit Gift Acceptance Policies," Strategic Alliance, www.giftplanners.com/pdfs/understanding.pdf.

93. "Employment Law Guide: Laws, Regulations, and Technical Assistance Services," U.S. Department of Labor, www.dol.gov/compliance/guide/index.htm.

94. "Employment Law Guide for Non-Profit Organizations," ProBono Partnership, www.probonopartner.org/PBPGuide/frame.htm.

95. "FirstStep Employment Law Advisor," U.S. Department of Labor, www.dol .gov/elaws/firststep.

96. Carter McNamara, ed., "Checklist of Human Resource Management Indicators for Nonprofit Organizations," Free Management Library, www.managementhelp.org/ org_eval/uw_hr.htm.

97. "Coverage," U.S. Equal Employment Opportunity Commission, www.eeoc.gov/ employers/coverage.cfm.

98. ProBono Partnership, "Employment Law Guide."

99. ProBono Partnership, "Employment Law Guide"; see appendix 1.

100. "Employers," U.S. Equal Employment Opportunity Commission, www.eeoc .gov/employers/index.cfm.

101. "Ethnic/National Origin, Color, Race, Religion & Sex Discrimination," U.S. Department of Labor, www.dol.gov/dol/topic/discrimination/ethnicdisc.htm.

102. "Age Discrimination," U.S. Department of Labor, www.dol.gov/dol/topic/discrimination/agedisc.htm.

103. ProBono Partnership, "Employment Law Guide."

104. "Hiring Youth," U.S. Department of Labor, www.dol.gov/compliance/topics/hiring-youth.htm.

105. "Americans with Disabilities Act," U.S. Department of Labor, www.dol.gov/dol/topic/disability/ada.htm.

106. "Disability Resources," U.S. Department of Labor, www.dol.gov/dol/topic/disability/employersresponsibilities.htm.

107. "Guidance on the Genetic Information Nondiscrimination Act," U.S. Department of Health and Human Services, www.hhs.gov/ohrp/humansubjects/guidance/gina.html.

108. "Genetic Information Discrimination," U.S. Equal Employment Opportunity Commission, www.eeoc.gov/laws/types/genetic.cfm.

109. ProBono Partnership, "Employment Law Guide."

110. "The Uniformed Services Employment and Reemployment Rights Act (USERRA)," U.S. Department of Labor, www.dol.gov/compliance/laws/comp-userra.htm.

111. "Immigration," U.S. Department of Labor, www.dol.gov/dol/topic/discrimination/immdisc.htm.

112. ProBono Partnership, "Employment Law Guide."

113. "Affirmative Action," U.S. Department of Labor, www.dol.gov/dol/topic/hiring/affirmativeact.htm.

114. Aaron Larson, "Sexual Harassment Law," ExpertLaw, www.expertlaw.com/library/employment/sexual_harassment.html.

115. "Facts about Sexual Harassment," U.S. Equal Employment Opportunity Commission, www.eeoc.gov/facts/fs-sex.html.

116. U.S. Equal Employment Opportunity Commission, "Facts about Sexual Harassment."

117. Larson, "Sexual Harassment Law."

118. "Policy Guidance on Current Issues of Sexual Harassment," U.S. Equal Employment Opportunity Commission, www.eeoc.gov/policy/docs/currentissues.html.

119. "Whistleblower Protections," U.S. Department of Labor, www.dol.gov/compliance/laws/comp-whistleblower.htm.

120. "Employment at Will: What Does It Mean?" Nolo, www.nolo.com/legal-encyclopedia/employment-at-will-definition-30022.html.

121. "Employment at Will States," EmployeeIssues.com, http://employeeissues.com/at_will_states.htm.

122. "Fair Labor Standards Act (FLSA)," U.S. Department of Labor, www.dol.gov/whd/flsa/index.htm.

123. "Minimum Wage," U.S. Department of Labor, www.dol.gov/whd/minimumwage.htm.

124. "Breaks & Meal Periods," U.S. Department of Labor, www.dol.gov/dol/topic/workhours/breaks.htm.

125. "Travel Time," U.S. Department of Labor, www.dol.gov/dol/topic/workhours/traveltime.htm.

126. "Health Benefits," U.S. Department of Labor, www.dol.gov/compliance/topics/benefits-health.htm.

127. "Workers' Compensation," U.S. Department of Labor, www.dol.gov/dol/topic/workcomp/index.htm.

128. "State Workers' Compensation Offices," Business.gov, www.business.gov/business-law/employment/workers-compensation/state-workers-compensation .html?cm_re=WorkersCompensationbyState-_-NULL-_-NULL.

129. "Leave Benefits," U.S. Department of Labor, www.dol.gov/dol/topic/benefits -leave/index.htm.

130. "Family & Medical Leave," U.S. Department of Labor, www.dol.gov/dol/topic/benefits-leave/fmla.htm.

131. "Continuation of Health Coverage—COBRA," U.S. Department of Labor, www.dol.gov/dol/topic/health-plans/cobra.htm.

132. "Portability of Health Coverage," U.S. Department of Labor, www.dol.gov/dol/topic/health-plans/portability.htm.

133. "Termination," U.S. Department of Labor, www.dol.gov/dol/topic/termination/index.htm.

134. Phelan, *Museums and the Law*, 148–51.

135. U.S. Department of Labor, "Fair Labor Standards Act."

136. "Recordkeeping & Reporting," U.S. Department of Labor, www.dol.gov/dol/topic/workhours/hoursrecordkeeping.htm.

137. "Employee Retirement Income Security Act (ERISA)," U.S. Department of Labor, www.dol.gov/dol/topic/retirement/erisa.htm.

138. Alberta Museums Association, *Standard Practices Handbook for Museums*, 2nd ed. (Edmonton, Alberta: Alberta Museums Association, 1990), 105–6.

139. For information on finding and contracting with such groups, see "Contracted Service by Type," American Association of Museums, www.aam-us.org/museumresources/ic/hr/cs/bytype.cfm.

140. "Independent Contractor (Self-Employed) or Employee?" Internal Revenue Service, www.irs.gov/businesses/small/article/0,,id=99921,00.html.

141. Internal Revenue Service, "Independent Contractor (Self-Employed) or Employee?"

142. "Employment Relationship under the Fair Labor Standards Act (FLSA)," U.S. Department of Labor, www.dol.gov/whd/regs/compliance/whdfs13.pdf.

143. Volunteer Protection Act, Public Law 105-19, 105th Congress (June 18, 1997), available on the Nebraska Department of Insurance website at www.doi.ne.gov/shiip/volunteer/pl_105.19.pdf.

144. "State Liability Laws for Charitable Organizations and Volunteers," Nonprofit Risk Management Center, http://nonprofitrisk.org/downloads/state-liability.pdf.

145. Volunteer Protection Act.

146. See the Nonprofit Risk Management Center, "State Liability Laws," 16–124, for a state-by-state list of volunteer liability laws.

147. Joan Kuyper, *Volunteer Program Administration: A Handbook for Museums and Other Cultural Institutions* (New York: American Council for the Arts in association with the American Association for Museum Volunteers, 1993), 20–21.

148. Nonprofit Risk Management Center, "State Liability Laws."

149. Kuyper, *Volunteer Program Administration*, 17–18.

150. Sanna Wolk, "Intellectual Property Law and Ownership in Employment Relationships," Sanna Wolk, www.wolk.se/Publikationer/Employee%20IPR_Kap05.pdf, 2.

151. Rina Elster Pantalony, "WIPO Guide on Managing Intellectual Property for Museums," World Intellectual Property Organization, August 2007, www.wipo.int/copyright/en/museums_ip/guide.html.

152. "Human Resources Software: Legal Issues," Auxillium West, www.auxillium.com/records.shtml.

153. "Recordkeeping Requirements," Business Owner's Toolkit, www.toolkit.com/small_business_guide/sbg.aspx?nid=P05_4077.

154. "Sample Document Retention and Destruction Policy," Volunteer Lawyers & Accountants for the Arts, www.vlaa.org/assets/documents/Sample%20Document%20Retention%20and%20Destruction%20Policy.doc.

155. "Electronic Records Management Guidelines," Minnesota Historical Society, www.mnhs.org/preserve/records/electronicrecords/erguidelines.html.

156. "Electronic Records: Treating Email As Records." Smithsonian Institution Archives, http://siarchives.si.edu/records/records_erecords_emailrecords2.html.

157. Menzi L. Behrnd-Klodt, *Navigating Legal Issues in Archives* (Chicago: Society of American Archivists, 2008), 191–92.

158. Malaro, *A Legal Primer*, 65.

159. Malaro, *A Legal Primer*, 66.

160. Malaro, *A Legal Primer*, 67–84.

161. Malaro, *A Legal Primer*, 84–118.

162. Sherry Hutt, Caroline M. Blanco, and Ole Varmer, *Heritage Resources Law: Protecting the Archeological and Cultural Environment* (New York: John Wiley & Sons, 1999).

163. "Guidelines Concerning the Unlawful Appropriation of Objects during the Nazi Era," American Association of Museums, www.aam-us.org/museumresources/ethics/nazi_guidelines.cfm.

164. "Nazi Era Provenance," American Association of Museums, www.aam-us.org/museumresources/prov/index.cfm.

165. "American Antiquities Act of 1906," National Park Service, www.nps.gov/history/local-law/anti1906.htm.

166. Malaro, *A Legal Primer*, 128–29.

167. "Convention for the Protection of Cultural Property in the Event of Armed Conflict with Regulations for the Execution of the Convention 1954," UNESCO, http://portal.unesco.org/en/ev.php-URL_ID=13637&URL_DO=DO_TOPIC&URL_SECTION=201.html.

168. Alberta Museums Association, *Standard Practices Handbook*, 165.

169. Malaro, *A Legal Primer*, 88–93, 103–10.

170. "National Historic Preservation Act of 1966, As Amended through 2006," Advisory Council on Historic Preservation, www.achp.gov/docs/nhpa%202008-final.pdf.

171. Malaro, *A Legal Primer*, 131–32.

172. "Archaeological Resources Protection Act of 1979," National Park Service, www.nps.gov/history/local-law/fhpl_ArchRsrcsProt.pdf.

173. Malaro, *A Legal Primer*, 129–30.

174. "Convention on Stolen or Illegally Exported Cultural Objects," UNIDROIT, www.unidroit.org/english/conventions/1995culturalproperty/1995culturalproperty-e.htm.

175. Malaro, *A Legal Primer*, 105–6.

176. National NAGPRA, "Law, Regulations, and Guidance," National Parks Service, www.nps.gov/nagpra/MANDATES/INDEX.HTM.

177. See National NAGPRA at www.nps.gov/nagpra.

178. Thomas F. King, *Cultural Resource Laws & Practice: An Introductory Guide*, 2nd ed. (Walnut Creek, CA: AltaMira Press, 2004), 192–201.

179. Malaro, *A Legal Primer*, 112–17.

180. "Convention on the Protection of the Underwater Cultural Heritage," UNESCO, http://unesdoc.unesco.org/images/0012/001260/126065e.pdf.

181. Alberta Museums Association, *Standard Practices Handbook*, 165.

182. "Convention on International Trade in Endangered Species of Wild Fauna and Flora," CITES, www.cites.org/eng/disc/text.shtml.

183. "Lacy Act," U.S. Department of Agriculture, Animal and Plant Health Inspection Service, www.aphis.usda.gov/plant_health/lacey_act/index.shtml.

184. Malaro, *A Legal Primer*, 120–21.

185. "Digest of Federal Resource Laws of Interest to the U.S. Fish and Wildlife Service," U.S. Fish and Wildlife Service, www.fws.gov/laws/lawsdigest/migtrea.html.

186. Malaro, *A Legal Primer*, 123.

187. "Bald Eagle Management Guidelines and Conservation Measures," U.S. Fish and Wildlife Service, www.fws.gov/midwest/Eagle/guidelines/bgepa.html.

188. Malaro, *A Legal Primer*, 123.

189. "The Marine Mammal Protection Act of 1972 As Amended," National Oceanic and Atmospheric Administration, National Marine Fisheries Service, www.nmfs.noaa.gov/pr/pdfs/laws/mmpa.pdf.

190. "Marine Mammal Protection Act (MMPA) of 1972," National Oceanic and Atmospheric Administration, National Marine Fisheries Service, www.nmfs.noaa.gov/pr/laws/mmpa.

191. Malaro, *A Legal Primer*, 122–23.

192. "Laws and Policies," National Oceanic and Atmospheric Administration (NOAA), National Marine Fisheries Service, www.nmfs.noaa.gov/pr/laws.

193. Malaro, *A Legal Primer*, 121.

194. NOAA, "Laws and Policies."

195. Malaro, *A Legal Primer*, 122.

196. "Antarctic Conservation Act," National Science Foundation, www.nsf.gov/od/opp/antarct/aca/aca.jsp.

197. Malaro, *A Legal Primer*, 124–25.

198. "African Elephant Conservation Act of 1989," U.S. Fish and Wildlife Service, Division of Management and Scientific Authorities, www.fws.gov/international/laws/aeca_fv.html.

199. Malaro, *A Legal Primer*, 124.

200. "Digest of Federal Resource Laws of Interest to the U.S. Fish and Wildlife Service," U.S. Fish and Wildlife Service, www.fws.gov/laws/lawsdigest/wildbrd.html.

201. Malaro, *A Legal Primer*, 124.

202. Phelan, *Museums and the Law*, 99.

203. Malaro, *A Legal Primer*, 136.

204. Malaro, *A Legal Primer*, 135–49.

205. "Charitable Contributions: Substantiation and Disclosure Requirements," Publication 1771, Internal Revenue Service, www.irs.gov/pub/irs-pdf/p1771.pdf.

206. "UCC: Uniform Commercial Code," Cornell University Law School, Legal Information Institute, www.law.cornell.edu/ucc/ucc.table.html.

207. Phelan, *Museums and the Law*, 94–98; Malaro, *A Legal Primer*, 68–71.

208. "Sales and Other Disposition of Assets," Publication 544, Internal Revenue Service, www.irs.gov/publications/p544/ch01.html.

209. See Arabella Yip, "Bargain Sales: Too Good to Be True?" *Art Law Clinic Client Newsletter* (Fall 2005): 4–5, www.law.harvard.edu/academics/clinical/lsc/pdf/Art%20Law%20Clinic%20Newsletter1.pdf. See also Malaro, *A Legal Primer*, 377–78.

210. Timothy Ambrose and Crispin Paine, *Museum Basics*, 2nd ed. (New York: Routledge, 2006), 302.

211. Malaro, *A Legal Primer*, 62–64.

212. For more on bailments and a museum's liability exposure on incoming loans, see Malaro, *A Legal Primer*, 240–41.

213. For more on insurance to cover incoming loans, see Malaro, *A Legal Primer*, 241–44.

214. Malaro, *A Legal Primer*, 248–52.

215. Malaro, *A Legal Primer*, 259.

216. For more on outgoing loans and insurance, including setting values on objects, see Malaro, *A Legal Primer*, 259–73.

217. Malaro, *A Legal Primer*, 284–314.

218. Malaro, *A Legal Primer*, 350.

219. Malaro, *A Legal Primer*, 349–54.

220. Malaro, *A Legal Primer*, 355.

221. Malaro, *A Legal Primer*, 355–59.

222. "§ 170. Charitable, etc., Contributions and Gifts," Cornell University Law School, Legal Information Institute, www.law.cornell.edu/uscode/26/usc_sec_26_00000170----000-.html.

223. Phelan, *Museums and the Law*, 101–2.

224. "Determining the Value of Donated Property," Publication 561, Internal Revenue Service, www.irs.gov/publications/p561/ar02.html#d0e139.

225. Malaro, *A Legal Primer*, 370–71.

226. Malaro, *A Legal Primer*, 207n400.

227. Malaro, *A Legal Primer*, 208–9 and 372–73.

228. Malaro, *A Legal Primer*, 384–86.

229. Malaro, *A Legal Primer*, 387–88.

230. "Noncash Charitable Contributions," Form 8283, Internal Revenue Service, www.irs.gov/pub/irs-pdf/f8283.pdf.

231. Malaro, *A Legal Primer*, 386–87.

232. Malaro, *A Legal Primer*, 394–96.

233. Malaro, *A Legal Primer*, 396.

234. Malaro, *A Legal Primer*, 399–402.

235. For information on trademarks, patents, and trade secrets, see, inter alia, Michael S. Shapiro and Brett I. Miller, *A Museum Guide to Copyright and Trademark* (Washington, DC: American Association of Museums, 1999), 59–92; Robert C. Lind, Robert M. Jarvis, and Marilyn E. Phelan, *Art and Museum Law: Cases and Materials* (Durham, NC: Carolina Academic Press, 2002), 99–122; section 2:40 of "Legal Issues," chapter 2 in *Museum Handbook*, National Park Service, www.nps.gov/history/museum/publications/MHIII/mh3ch2.pdf; the U.S. Patent and Trademark Office website at www.uspto.gov.

236. For the complete version of the copyright law, see "Copyright Law of the United States and Related Laws Contained in Title 17 of the United States Code," U.S. Copyright Office, www.copyright.gov/title17.

237. Shapiro and Miller, *A Museum Guide*, 18–21.

238. "Copyright Basics," U.S. Copyright Office, www.copyright.gov/circs/circ1.pdf.

239. U.S. Copyright Office, "Copyright Basics."

240. U.S. Copyright Office, "Copyright Basics."

241. Stephen C. Nill, "Do Volunteers Own the Copyright When They Contribute Creative Works?" Idealist, www.idealist.org/if/idealist/en/FAQ/QuestionViewer/default?section=16&item=40.

242. Nill, "Do Volunteers Own the Copyright."

243. Tables 4.3 and 4.4 are based, in part, on charts by Peter B. Hirtle, "Copyright Term and the Public Domain in the United States," Copyright Information Center, Cornell University, http://copyright.cornell.edu/resources/publicdomain.cfm (current as of January 1, 2010); Lolly Gasaway, "When U.S. Works Pass into the Public Domain," University of North Carolina, Chapel Hill, www.unc.edu/~unclng/public-d.htm; Malaro, *A Legal Primer*, 155–56; and Mary Minow, "Library Digitization Projects: U.S. Copyrighted Works That Have Expired into the Public Domain," LibraryLaw.com, www.librarylaw.com/DigitizationTable.htm. See also "Duration of Copyright: Provisions of the Law Dealing with the Length of Copyright Protection," Circular 15a, U.S. Copyright Office, 2004, www.copyright.gov/circs/circ15a.pdf. The chart does not include information on works or sound recordings published outside the

United States, "special cases," or architectural works; for these, see Hirtle, "Copyright Term and the Public Domain."

244. To learn more about the four factors and whether they apply to a use of copyrighted works, see Shapiro and Miller, *A Museum Guide*, 52–54.

245. "Reproduction of Copyrighted Works by Educators and Librarians," U.S. Copyright Office, www.copyright.gov/circs/circ21.pdf.

246. U.S. Copyright Office, "Reproduction of Copyrighted Works."

247. The information on sound recordings applies only to the sound recording itself, not to any copyrights in compositions or texts.

248. Shapiro and Miller, *A Museum Guide*, 55.

249. U.S. Copyright Office, "Copyright Law of the United States."

250. Shapiro and Miller, *A Museum Guide*, 28.

251. Shapiro and Miller, *A Museum Guide*, 28.

252. "Use of Videotapes/DVDs/Video Files," American Library Association, www.ala.org/ala/professionalresources/libfactsheets/alalibraryfactsheet07.cfm.

253. "Fair Use of Copyrighted Materials," University of Texas System, www.utsystem.edu/OGC/IntellectualProperty/copypol2.htm.

254. See the Copyright Clearance Center website at www.copyright.com.

255. See University of Texas System, "Fair Use of Copyrighted Materials," for a list of organizations to contact.

256. Rachel Durkin, "Obtaining Rights to Produce a Play or Musical or Use Music in Live Performances," University of Texas System, www.utsystem.edu/OGC/IntellectualProperty/perform.htm.

257. See the websites for the Motion Picture Licensing Company (www.mplc.com), Movie Licensing USA (www.movlic.com), and Swank Motion Pictures, Inc. (www.swank.com).

258. "Getting Permission," University of Texas System, www.utsystem.edu/OGC/IntellectualProperty/permissn.htm.

259. John A. Neuenschwander, *A Guide to Oral History and the Law* (New York: Oxford University Press, 2009).

260. See the Oral History Association website at www.oralhistory.org.

261. "Oral History Evaluation Guidelines," Oral History Association, www.oralhistory.org/do-oral-history/oral-history-evaluation-guidelines.

262. Neuenschwander, *A Guide to Oral History*, 115–30.

263. Neuenschwander, *A Guide to Oral History*, 5.

264. Neuenschwander, *A Guide to Oral History*, 19–48, 87–96, 105–12.

265. Linda Shopes, "Human Subjects and IRB Review: Oral History, Human Subjects, and Institutional Review Boards," Oral History Association, www.oralhistory.org/do-oral-history/oral-history-and-irb-review.

266. National Park Service, "Legal Issues."

267. "Preventive conservation can be defined as any measure that prevents damage or reduces the potential for it. It focuses on collections rather than individual objects, nontreatment rather than treatment." "Preventive Conservation," *Conservation* 7, no. 1 (winter 1992), as quoted in Malaro, *A Legal Primer*, 413.

268. Malaro, *A Legal Primer*, 408–9.

269. "Conservation Assessment Program," Institute of Museum and Library Services, www.imls.gov/applicants/grants/conservAssessment.shtm.

270. Malaro, *A Legal Primer*, 420.

271. Malaro, *A Legal Primer*, 420.

272. Malaro, *A Legal Primer*, 418–32.

273. American Association for State and Local History (AASLH), *StEPs: Standards and Excellence Program for History Organizations* (Nashville, TN: AASLH, 2009), 142; "Information Center Fact Sheet: Ethics of Deaccessioning," American Association of Museums, www.aam-us.org/museumresources/ic/cs/cm/deaccess/loader.cfm?url=/commonspot/security/getfile.cfm&PageID=4052.

274. Malaro, *A Legal Primer*, 219.

275. Malaro, *A Legal Primer*, 228.

276. Malaro, *A Legal Primer*, 229.

277. Malaro, *A Legal Primer*, 235.

278. Malaro, *A Legal Primer*, 238.

279. National Park Service, "Legal Issues."

280. "Privacy Act of 1984," Federal Trade Commission, www.ftc.gov/foia/privacy_act.shtm.

281. Menzi L. Behrnd-Klodt, *Navigating Legal Issues in Archives*. (Chicago: Society of American Archivists, 2008), 101–65.

282. Deborah Wythe, ed., *Museum Archives: An Introduction*, 2nd ed. (Chicago: Society of American Archivists, 2004), 57–58.

283. "Freedom of Information Act," U.S. Department of Justice, www.justice.gov/oip/foia_guide07/text_foia.pdf.

284. Malaro, *A Legal Primer*, 440.

285. National Park Service, "Legal Issues," figure 2.1.

286. Frank B. Cross and Roger LeRoy Miller, *The Legal Environment of Business: Text and Cases* (Florence, KY: Cengage Learning, 2008), 624.

287. "Charitable Contributions," Publication 526, Internal Revenue Service, www.irs.gov/pub/irs-pdf/p526.pdf

288. Barry G. Szczesny, "Are Museum Memberships Tax Deductible?" *Museum News* (November–December 2003), www.aam-us.org/pubs/mn/MN_ND03_LawEthics.cfm.

289. Association of Direct Response Fundraising Counsel, "What Your Organization Needs to Know about Direct Mail Fundraising," Carl Bloom Associates, 2000, www.carlbloom.com/marketing/dmfund.html.

290. U.S. Department of Justice, "Americans with Disabilities Act of 1990, As Amended," ADA Home Page, www.ada.gov/pubs/ada.htm.

291. For excerpts of the Telecommunications Act of 1996 relating to disability issues, see the Trace Center website at http://trace.wisc.edu/docs/taacmtg_jun96/excerpts.htm.

292. U.S. Department of Justice, "Americans with Disabilities Act."

293. Malaro, *A Legal Primer*, 446.

294. Malaro, *A Legal Primer*, 447.

295. Malaro, *A Legal Primer*, 446.

296. Thomas C. Jester and Sharon C. Park, "Making Historic Properties Accessible," Preservation Brief 32, National Park Service, 1993, www.nps.gov/history/hps/tps/briefs/brief32.htm.

297. National Assembly of State Arts Agencies, *Design for Accessibility: A Cultural Administrator's Handbook*, National Endowment for the Arts, www.arts.gov/resources/Accessibility/pubs/DesignAccessibility.html; see especially chapter 2, "Legal Overview: The ADA and the Rehabilitation Act."

298. U.S. Department of Justice, "Americans with Disabilities Act Homepage," www.ada.gov. The toll-free ADA information line, to obtain answers to general and technical questions about the ADA, is 800-514-0301 (voice) 800-514-0383 (TTY).

299. "State Code Contact List," U.S. Access Board, www.access-board.gov/links/statecodes.htm.

300. Geoffrey G. Gussis, "Auditing the Non-Profit Website." ProBono Partnership, 2002, www.probonopartner.org/publications/auditing%20website.htm.

301. Gussis, "Auditing the Non-Profit Website."

302. "Right of Privacy: An Overview," Cornell University Law School, Legal Information Institute, http://topics.law.cornell.edu/wex/privacy.

303. "How to Comply with Children's Online Privacy Protection Act," Children's Online Privacy Protection Act, www.coppa.org/comply.htm.

304. "A Primer on Invasion of Privacy," Reporters Committee for Freedom of the Press, www.rcfp.org/photoguide/intro.html.

305. "9 Keys to Avoiding Invasion of Privacy Suits," Reporters Committee for Freedom of the Press, www.rcfp.org/photoguide/ninekeys.html.

306. "What Is a Release?" Center for Internet and Society Fair Use Project, Stanford University Libraries and Academic Information Resources, http://fairuse.stanford.edu/Copyright_and_Fair_Use_Overview/chapter12/12-a.html.

307. F. Howie, ed., *Safety in Museums and Galleries* (Boston: Butterworths, 1987), 29.

308. "Nonprofit CARES," Nonprofit Risk Management Center, http://nonprofitrisk.org/tools/cares/cares.shtml.

309. See the Nonprofit Risk Management Center website at http://nonprofitrisk.org.

310. Claire Lee Reiss, "Risk Identification and Analysis: A Guide for Small Public Entities," Public Entity Risk Institute, www.riskinstitute.org/peri/images/file/RiskID_Full.pdf.

311. Melanie Lockwood Herman, "Preventing and Responding to Fraud and Misuse of Assets in a Nonprofit Organization," Nonprofit Risk Management Center, http://nonprofitrisk.org/library/articles/internalcontrol05062001.shtml.

312. Hurwit, "Nonprofit Governance."

313. Diane Adams-Graf and Claudia J. Nicholson, "Thinking Ahead about Museum Protection: An Ounce of Prevention Is Worth a Pound of Cure," Minnesota Historical Society, *Tech Talk*, 2000, www.mnhs.org/about/publications/techtalk/TechTalkMarch2000.pdf.

314. Museum, Library, and Cultural Properties Council of ASIS International and Museum Association Security Committee of AAM, "Suggested Practices for Museum

Security," American Association of Museums, www.aam-us.org/museumresources/ic/frm/rm/loader.cfm?url=/commonspot/security/getfile.cfm&PageID=25668.

315. Malaro, *A Legal Primer*, 412.

316. "Occupational Safety and Health Act of 1970," Occupational Safety and Health Administration, www.osha.gov/pls/oshaweb/owasrch.search_form?p_doc_type=oshact.

317. "Material Data Safety Sheets," James R. Macdonald Laboratory, Kansas State University, http://jrm.phys.ksu.edu/safety/msds.html.

318. For additional hazards often found in collections, see "Information Center Fact Sheet: Hazards in Collections," American Association of Museums, www.aam-us.org/museumresources/ic/frm/rm/loader.cfm?url=/commonspot/security/getfile.cfm&PageID=2440.

319. Malaro, *A Legal Primer*, 452.

320. "Federal Insecticide, Fungicide, and Rodenticide Act (FIFRA)," U.S. Environmental Protection Agency, www.epa.gov/oecaagct/lfra.html.

321. Malaro, *A Legal Primer*, 416.

322. "Disaster Plan Development," American Association of Museums, www.aam-us.org/museumresources/ic/frm/rm/plan.cfm.

323. "Emergency Preparedness & Recovery," American Association of Museums, www.aam-us.org/museumresources/ic/frm/rm/epr.

324. Malaro, *A Legal Primer*, 417.

325. "National Preservation Law of 1966," National Park Service, www.nps.gov/history/local-law/nhpa1966.htm.

326. "The Secretary of the Interior's Standards for the Treatment of Historic Properties," National Park Service, 1995, www.nps.gov/history/local-law/arch_stnds_8_2.htm.

327. "Tax Incentives," National Park Service, www.nps.gov/history/tax.htm.

328. "Codes, Standards, and Guidelines," International Code Council, www.iccsafe.org/Pages/default.aspx.

329. "Codes and Standards," National Fire Protection Association, www.nfpa.org/categoryList.asp?categoryID=124&URL=Codes%20&%20Standards.

330. See, inter alia, "NFPA 914: Code for Fire Protection of Historic Structures," National Fire Protection Association, www.nfpa.org/aboutthecodes/AboutTheCodes.asp?DocNum=914.

331. Harriet Whelchel, ed. *Caring for Your Historic House* (New York: Harry N. Abrams, 1998), 213–14.

332. "Elevator Law and Legal Definition," USLegal, http://definitions.uslegal.com/e/elevator.

333. "Codes and Standards," National Elevator Industry, Inc., www.neii.org/codes.cfm.

334. John R. Luckey, "The United States Flag: Federal Law Relating to Display and Associated Questions," U.S. Senate, Congressional Research Service, 2008, www.senate.gov/reference/resources/pdf/RL30243.pdf.

INDEX

ABOUT THE EDITORS

Cinnamon Catlin-Legutko has worked in the small museum world since 1994 and was the director of the General Lew Wallace Study & Museum in Crawfordsville, Indiana, from 2003 to 2009. In 2008, the museum was awarded the National Medal for Museum Service. Her contributions to the field include leadership of the AASLH Small Museums Committee, service as an IMLS grant reviewer and AAM MAP peer reviewer, and service as an AASLH Council member. She is now CEO of the Abbe Museum in Bar Harbor, Maine.

Stacy Klingler currently serves local history organizations as the assistant director of local history services at the Indiana Historical Society. She began her career in museums as the assistant director of two small museums, before becoming director of the Putnam County Museum in Greencastle, Indiana. She chairs the AASLH's Small Museums Committee (2008–2012) and attended the Seminar for Historical Administration in 2006. While she lives in the history field, her passion is encouraging a love of learning in any environment.

ABOUT THE CONTRIBUTORS

Brenda Granger has worked for small museums and has been the executive director of the Oklahoma Museums Association (OMA) since 2005. The OMA supports the efforts of Oklahoma museums with their efforts to educate, inform, and entertain. Oklahoma is home to more than five hundred museums, with 75 percent of them being self-defined as small.

Benjamin Hruska is a PhD candidate in public history at Arizona State University. Before returning to graduate school, Hruska served as director of the Block Island Historical Society on Block Island, Rhode Island, and successfully obtained a building grant from the Rhode Island Historical Preservation & Heritage Commission. In the summer of 2009, he worked as a court historian for the Department of Defense's U.S. Court of Appeals for the Armed Forces in Washington, DC.

Allyn Lord is the director of the Shiloh Museum of Ozark History in Springdale, Arkansas. Since 1982 she has served on the AAM board; been an accreditation and Museum Assessment Program peer reviewer and an Institute of Museum and Library Services (IMLS) grant reviewer; and worked on numerous committees, including those serving small museums with both AAM and AASLH. She has also been active in the Arkansas Museums Association and Southeastern Museums Conference. She believes in the power of networking, professional development, mentoring, and service to the field.